Teacher's Resource Book

CONTENTS

Welcome to School!

CONTENTS

Hooray! It's Time for School

lyrics by Jenny Reznick and Becky Manfredini
music by Harry Manfredini

Newsletter

Welcome to School!

Dear Family,

This week _____ will introduce herself/himself to her/his classmates. Using the topic "All About Me," we will read stories about feelings and how people express them. You can help your child learn more by talking with her/him about the things he/she is doing at school and the new letters and words that he/she is learning. Here are some ways that you can work with your child at home.

Think & Talk

What did you read about today?
What feelings did you talk about?
How do you feel when you go to school?

Home Activities

Letters Everywhere

Find things your child uses at home that have print on them, such as a tube of toothpaste, a game, or a toy. Point out and name some of the letters. Ask your child to repeat the letter names.

How Do You Feel Today?

Cut out sets of happy and sad faces and put them in an envelope or small box. Ask your child how he/she feels each day after school. Have her/him pick out a happy or sad face and tape it to the appropriate day on a family calendar.

What I Learned

Here is a note from your child and her/his teacher

Spanish Newsletter

Welcome to School!

Querida familia:

Esta semana _____ va a presentarse a sus compañeros. Usando el tema "All About Me" ("Todo sobre mí"), leeremos cuentos sobre los sentimientos y las formas como las personas los expresan. Ustedes pueden ayudar a su niño o niña a aprender más hablándole sobre las cosas que está haciendo en la escuela y sobre las nuevas letras y palabras que está aprendiendo. A continuación hay algunas actividades que le pueden servir para trabajar con su hijo o hija en casa.

Pensar y conversar

¿Sobre qué leíste hoy?

¿De qué sentimientos hablaron en clase?

¿Cómo te sientes cuando estás en la escuela?

Actividades para la casa

Letras en todas partes

Busquen objetos que su hijo o hija usa y que tengan textos impresos. Puede ser un tubo de pasta de dientes, un juego o un juguete. Señalen y digan el nombre de algunas de las letras. Pidan al niño o niña que las repita.

¿Cómo te sientes?

Recorten grupos de caras felices y tristes, y pónganlas en un sobre o en una caja pequeña. Pregunten a su niño o niña cómo se siente después de la escuela y pidan que seleccione la cara correspondiente. Péguenla en al día correspondiente de un calendario.

Lo que aprendí

Lean la nota que escribimos juntos.

Newsletter

WEEK 2

Welcome to School!

Dear Family,

This week _____ will learn about friends and friendship. Using the topic "Let's Be Friends," we will read stories about making friends and how they work and play together. You can help your child learn more by talking with her/him about the things he/she is doing at school and the new letters and words that he/she is learning. Here are some ways that you can work with your child at home.

 Think & Talk

Did you meet someone new today?
Did you make any friends today?
What do you like to do with your friends?

Home Activities

Letters All Around Us

Write your child's first name on a piece of paper. Point out and name the first letter in her/his name. Name the rest of the letters in your child's name. Have your child trace the letters with her/his finger.

Where Is It?

Your child is learning position words, such as *above, below, top, middle, bottom, beside,* and *next to.* Help her/him practice using these words. Play a game in which you use the position words to tell your child where to put an object.

What I Learned

Here is a note from your child and her/his teacher.

Spanish Newsletter

WEEK 2

Welcome to School!

Querida familia:

Esta semana _____ aprenderá sobre los amigos y la amistad. Usando el tema "Let's Be Friends" ("Seamos amigos"), leeremos cuentos sobre cómo hacer amigos y las formas como ellos trabajan y juegan juntos. Ustedes pueden ayudar a su niño o niña a aprender más hablándole sobre las cosas que está haciendo en la escuela y sobre las nuevas letras y palabras que está aprendiendo. A continuación hay algunas actividades que le pueden servir para trabajar con su hijo o hija en casa.

Pensar y conversar

¿Conociste a alguien hoy?
¿Hiciste algunos amigos hoy?
¿Qué te gusta hacer con tus amigos?

Actividades para la casa

Letras alrededor

Escriban el nombre de su hijo en una hoja de papel. Señalen y digan el nombre de la primera letra del nombre. Mencionen el resto de las letras y hagan que el niño o niña las trace con su dedo.

¿Dónde está?

Su hijo o hija está aprendiendo palabras para indicar la posición, tales como *encima, debajo, arriba, en el medio, abajo, al lado* y *cerca de.* Ayúdenlo a practicar usar estas palabras. Jueguen a decirle dónde poner un objeto, usando estas palabras.

Lo que aprendí

Lean la nota que escribimos juntos.

Newsletter — WEEK 3

Welcome to School!

Dear Family,

This week _____ will learn about school. Using the topic "Our Happy Classroom," we will read stories about the many things we see and do at school. You can help your child learn more by talking with her/him about the things he/she is doing at school and the new letters and words that he/she is learning. Here are some ways that you can work with your child at home.

Think & Talk

What story did you read today?
What was the story about?
What shapes did you learn about?
Do you see any shapes at home? Where?

Home Activities

Name the Letters

Write the alphabet on a long strip of paper. Chant or sing the alphabet song as you point to each letter. Write the letters in your child's first name on index cards. Help your child identify each letter and match it to the appropriate letter on the alphabet strip.

Shape Hunt

Cut a rectangle, a circle, and a triangle out of construction paper. Have your child trace and name each shape. Take a walk around your neighborhood and look for these shapes on signs, houses, trees, or flowers.

What I Learned

Here is a note from your child and her/his teacher.

Spanish Newsletter

Welcome to School!

Querida familia:

Esta semana _____ aprenderá sobre la escuela. Usando el tema "Our Happy Classroom" ("Nuestra feliz clase"), leeremos cuentos sobre las muchas cosas que vemos y hacemos en la escuela. Ustedes pueden ayudar a su niño o niña a aprender más hablándole sobre las cosas que está haciendo en la escuela y sobre las nuevas letras y palabras que está aprendiendo. A continuación hay algunas actividades que le pueden servir para trabajar con su hijo o hija en casa.

Pensar y conversar

¿Qué cuento leíste hoy?
¿Sobre qué se trata?
¿Sobre qué formas aprendiste?
¿Ves algunas de esas formas aquí en casa? ¿Dónde?

Actividades para la casa

Nombra las letras

Escriban el alfabeto en una tira de papel. Reciten o canten la canción del alfabeto y señale cada letra. Escriban cada letra del nombre de su hijo o hija en una tarjeta. Ayúdenlo/a a que identifique cada letra y a que la encuentre en el alfabeto.

Buscando formas

Corten un triángulo, un círculo y un rectángulo de cartulina. Haga que su hijo o hija trace y nombre cada forma. Den una caminata por su vecindario y busquen estas formas en señales de tránsito, casas, árboles o flores.

Lo que aprendí

Lean la nota que escribimos juntos.

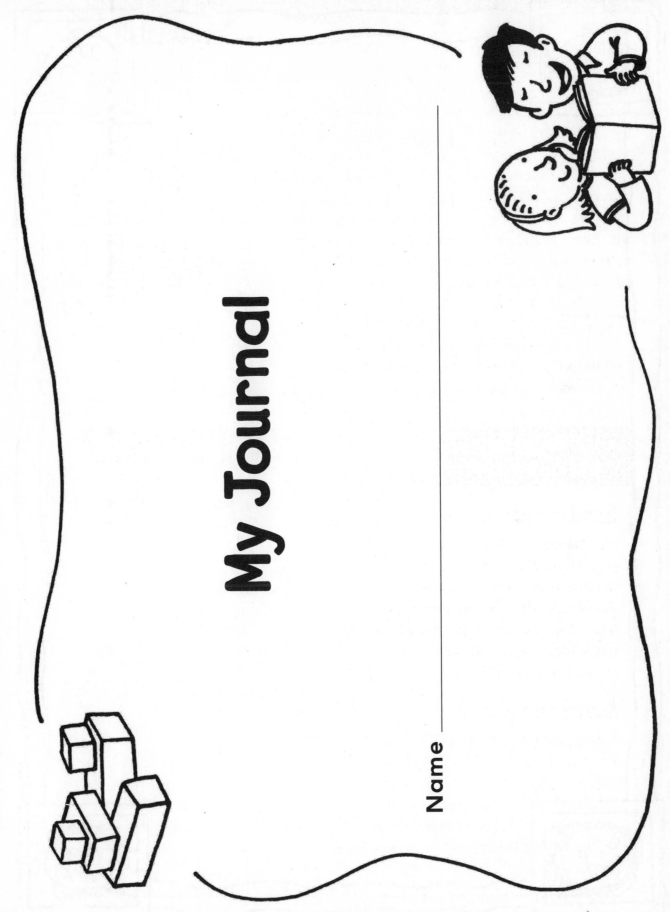

My Journal

Name _____

Border Paper

Shape Paper

Welcome to School!

Center Sign-Up Sheet

_____

_____

_____

_____

_____

_____

Story Retelling Props for *Lots of Feelings*

Story Retelling Props for *Lots of Feelings*

Story Retelling Props for "The Little Red Hen"

Story Retelling Props for "The Little Red Hen"

Story Retelling Props for *My Friend and I*

Story Retelling Props for *My Friend and I*

Story Retelling Props for "The Lion and the Mouse"

Story Retelling Props for "The Lion and the Mouse"

Story Retelling Props for *The Great Shape Hunt*

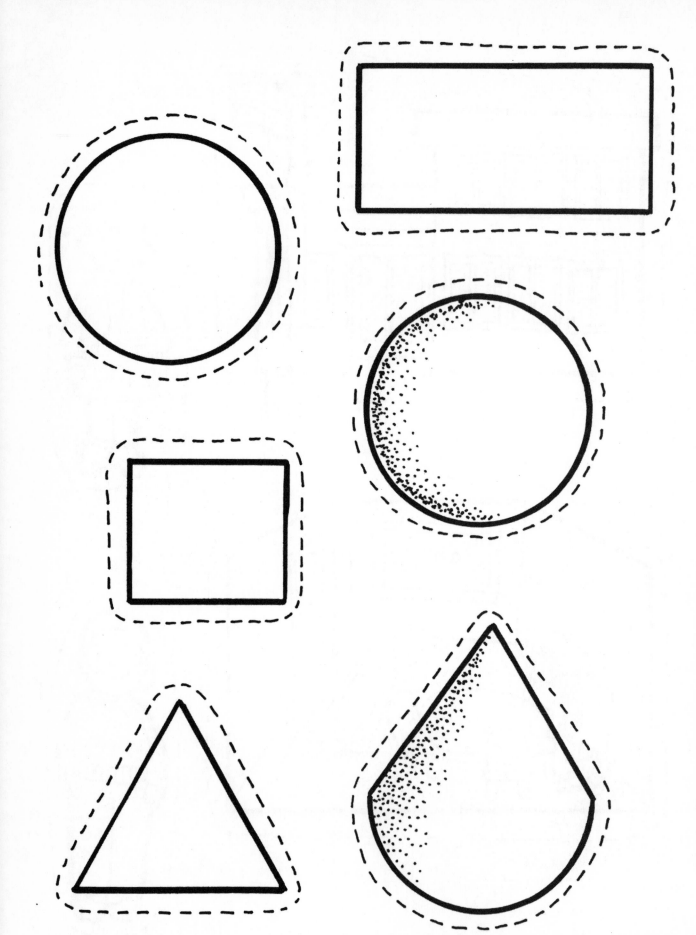

Story Retelling Props for *The Great Shape Hunt*

Story Retelling Props for "The Big-Mouth Frog"

THEME 1: Welcome to School!   **Story Retelling Props for "The Big-Mouth Frog"**

Theme 1: Welcome to School!

Houghton Mifflin
PRE-K
Where Bright Futures Begin!

Think & Talk

What's your favorite thing to do at school?

Time for School

Jared Kostka

ISBN 0-618513868

1-86110 LV PREK

HOUGHTON MIFFLIN

Title Code: 1-86110

COVER PhotoDisc/Getty Images. **2** Ellen Senisi/The Image Works. **3** Tom Pretty/PhotoEdit. **4** Picturequest. **5** Sean Justice/The Image Bank/ Getty Images. **6** Ellen Senisi/The Image Works. **7** Picturequest. **8** Ross Whitaker/ The Image Bank/ Getty Images. **9** Scholastic Studio 10/Index Stock.

Copyright (c) 2006 by Houghton Mifflin Company. All rights reserved. No part of this work may be reproduced or transmitted in any form or by any means, electronic or mechanical, including photocopying or recording, or by any information storage or retrieval system without the prior written permission of Houghton Mifflin Company unless such copying is expressly permitted by federal copyright law. Address inquiries to School Permissions, Houghton Mifflin Company, 222 Berkeley Street, Boston, MA 02116.

Printed in Mexico by RR Donnelley

ISBN: 0-618-51386-8

Time to go home!

9

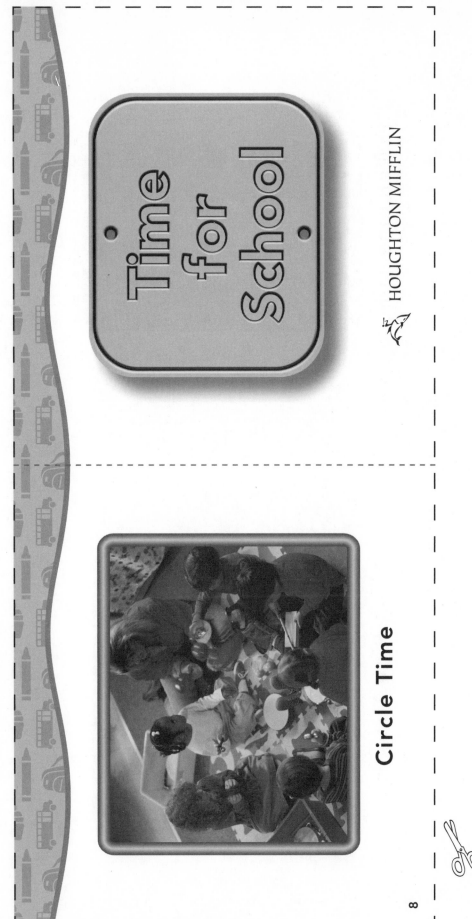

Time for School

HOUGHTON MIFFLIN

Circle Time

8

Welcome Time

Play Time

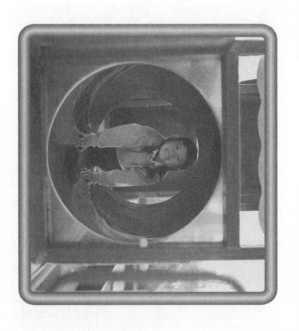

3

Meeting Time

Center Time

6

4

Story Time

Snack Time

5

Little Hands Library *Time for School*

boy

girl

school

teacher

happy

sad

friends

book

Picture-Word Cards

crayons

scissors

toys

diamond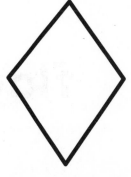

heart

star

quilt

flag

Picture-Word Cards

My Family, My Community

CONTENTS

My Family, My Community

lyrics by Jenny Reznick and Becky Manfredini
music by Harry Manfredini

moderate latin tempo

Verse 2
See us go to school each day.
See us in the park at play.
See us at the grocery store.
See our friends knock at our door.
If you look all around, I think you'll see—
My family's part of a community!

Verse 3
See the neighbors on our street.
See the people that we meet.
See everyone who cares for me.
They all help my family.
If you look all around, I think you'll see—
My family's part of a community!

Theme Song

Newsletter

My Family, My Community

Dear Family,

This week _____ will learn about families and all the members of a family. Using the topic "Meet My Family," we will read stories about things families do together. You can help your child learn more by talking with her/him about the things he/she is doing at school and the new letters and words that he/she is learning. Here are some ways that you can work with your child at home.

Think & Talk

What did you read today?
What was the story about?
Who are the people in our family?
What are some of the things that our family does together?

Home Activities

Letter Hunt

Look at book titles and newspaper or magazine headlines with your child to find letters of the alphabet. Start with the letter *A* and continue with the rest of the letters in *ABC* order. Encourage your child to name each letter as he/she finds it.

Morning Routines

Children will listen to a story about what each person in a family does in the morning. Ask your child to tell you about the things he/she does each morning. Prompt her/him to use the words *first*, *next*, and *last*.

What I Learned

Here is a note from your child and her/his teacher

Spanish Newsletter — WEEK 1

My Family, My Community

Querida familia:

Esta semana _____ aprenderá sobre las familias y los miembros de la familia. Usando el tema "Meet My Family" ("Conoce mi familia"), leeremos cuentos sobre las cosas que las familias hacen juntas. Ustedes pueden ayudar a su niño o niña a aprender más hablándole sobre las cosas que está haciendo en la escuela y sobre las nuevas letras y palabras que está aprendiendo. A continuación hay algunas actividades que le pueden servir para trabajar con su hijo o hija en casa.

Pensar y conversar

¿Qué leíste hoy?
¿Sobre qué se trata el cuento?
¿Quiénes son los miembros de nuestra familia?
¿Cuáles son algunas de las cosas que hacemos en familia?

Actividades para la casa

Buscando letras

Busquen con su hijo o hija las letras del alfabeto en los títulos de libros o en los titulares de periódicos o revistas. Empiecen con *A* y continúen con las demás en orden alfabético. Animen a su niño o niña a mencionar cada letra mientras las encuentre.

Rutinas de las mañanas

Los niños escucharán un cuento sobre lo que hace cada miembro de una familia en la mañana. Pidan a su hijo o hija que les cuente las cosas que hace cada mañana. Anímenlo a usar las palabras *primero, después* y *por último*.

Lo que aprendí

Lean la nota que escribimos juntos.

Newsletter — WEEK 2

My Family, My Community

Dear Family,

This week _____ will learn about neighbors and neighborhoods. Using the topic "Hello, Neighbor!" we will read stories about what it means to be a good neighbor. You can help your child learn more by talking with her/him about the things he/she is doing at school and the new letters and words that he/she is learning. Here are some ways that you can work with your child at home.

Think & Talk

What did you read today?
What was the story about?
Who lives in our neighborhood?
What things do you see in our neighborhood?

Home Activities

Ss Hunt

Page through newspaper or magazine headlines with your child, looking for capital *S* and small *s*. Circle the letters that you find. Look at the materials again and ask your child to point to each circled letter and say its name.

Sort Objects

Have your child sort objects in your home by size, shape, or color. Then have her/him count how many objects are in each set.

What I Learned

Here is a note from your child and her/his teacher.

Spanish Newsletter — WEEK 2

My Family, My Community

Querida familia:

Esta semana _____ aprenderá sobre los vecinos y los vecindarios. Usando el tema "Hello, Neighbor!" ("¡Hola, vecino!"), leeremos cuentos sobre lo que significa ser un buen vecino. Ustedes pueden ayudar a su niño o niña a aprender más hablándole sobre las cosas que está haciendo en la escuela y sobre las nuevas letras y palabras que está aprendiendo. A continuación hay algunas actividades que le pueden servir para trabajar con su hijo o hija en casa.

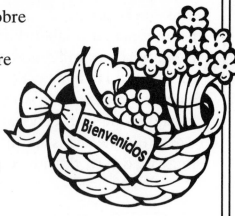

Pensar y conversar

¿Qué leíste hoy? ¿Sobre qué se trata el cuento?
¿Quiénes viven en nuestro vecindario?
¿Qué cosas ves en nuestro vecindario?

Actividades para la casa

Buscando *Ss*

Busquen con su hijo o hija las letras *S* mayúscula y *s* minúscula en titulares de periódicos o revistas. Encierren en un círculo cada letra que encuentren. Miren de nuevo el material y pidan a su niño o niña que señale cada letra encerrada y diga su nombre.

Clasificar objetos

Hagan que su hijo o hija clasifique objetos de su casa según su tamaño, forma y color. Pídanle que cuente cuántos objetos hay en cada grupo.

Lo que aprendí

Lean la nota que escribimos juntos.

Newsletter — WEEK 3

My Family, My Community

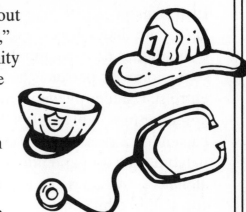

Dear Family,

This week _____ will learn about communities. Using the topic "Community Helpers," we will read stories about how people in a community help each other. You can help your child learn more by talking with her/him about the things he/she is doing at school and the new letters and words that he/she is learning. Here are some ways that you can work with your child at home.

Think & Talk

Who were the people in the story?
What do they do?
Do we have helpers in our community?
Who are they? What do they do?

Home Activities

Pp Card

Fold a piece of drawing paper in half. Write *Pp* on the front of the card. Name the letters and have your child repeat their names. Look for pictures of things that start with *Pp* in magazines or newspapers. Cut out the pictures and help your child glue them to the inside of the card.

Reading Together

Gather books about community helpers, such as firefighters, police officers, teachers, doctors, and nurses. Talk with your child about what the people pictured in the books do for others. Read the stories aloud to your child.

What I Learned

Here is a note from your child and her/his teacher.

Spanish Newsletter — WEEK 3

My Family, My Community

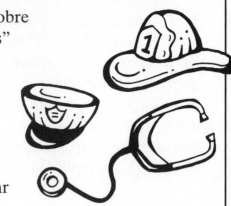

Querida familia:

Esta semana _____ aprenderá sobre las comunidades. Usando tema "Community Helpers" ("Ayudantes de la comunidad"), leeremos cuentos sobre cómo las personas de la comunidad se ayudan entre sí. Ustedes pueden ayudar a su niño o niña a aprender más hablándole sobre las cosas que está haciendo en la escuela y sobre las nuevas letras y palabras que está aprendiendo. A continuación hay algunas actividades que le pueden servir para trabajar con su hijo o hija en casa.

Pensar y conversar

¿Quiénes son las personas del cuento? ¿Qué hacen? ¿Tenemos ayudantes en nuestra comunidad? ¿Quiénes son? ¿Qué hacen ellos?

Actividades para la casa

La tarjeta de la *Pp*

Doblen por la mitad una hoja de papel. Escriban *Pp* en la parte de enfrente. Busquen en revistas o periódicos fotografías o dibujos de objetos cuyos nombres empiezan con *Pp*. Córtenlas y ayude a su hijo o hija a pegarlas en el interior de la tarjeta.

Leyendo juntos

Reúnan libros sobre los ayudantes de la comunidad, tales como los bomberos, policias, maestros, doctores y enfermeras. Hablen con su niño o niña sobre lo que hacen por otros las personas de los libros. Léanle los cuentos.

Lo que aprendí

Lean la nota que escribimos juntos.

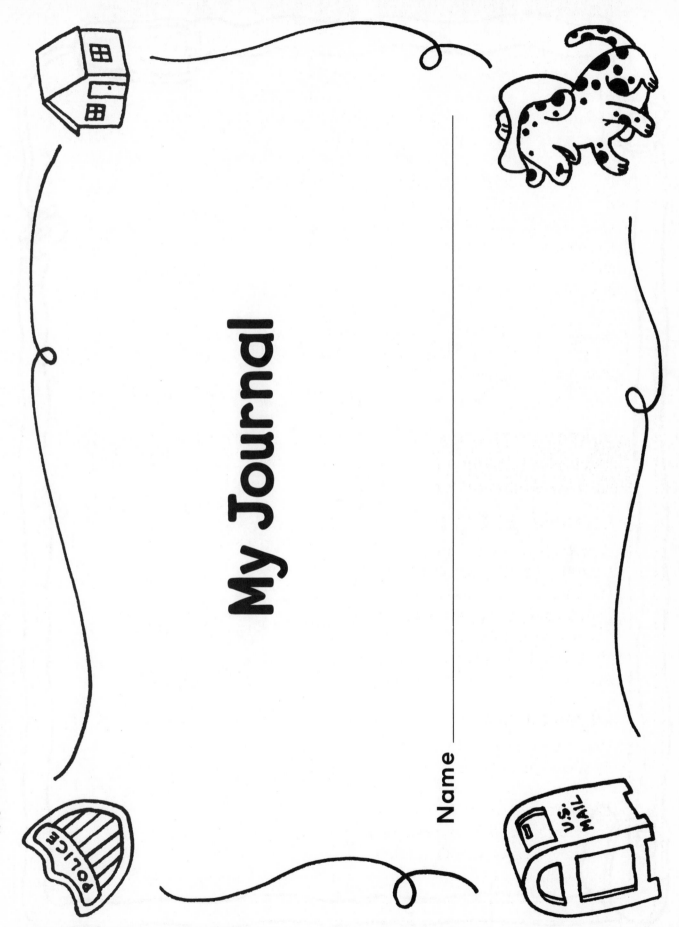

My Journal

Name _____

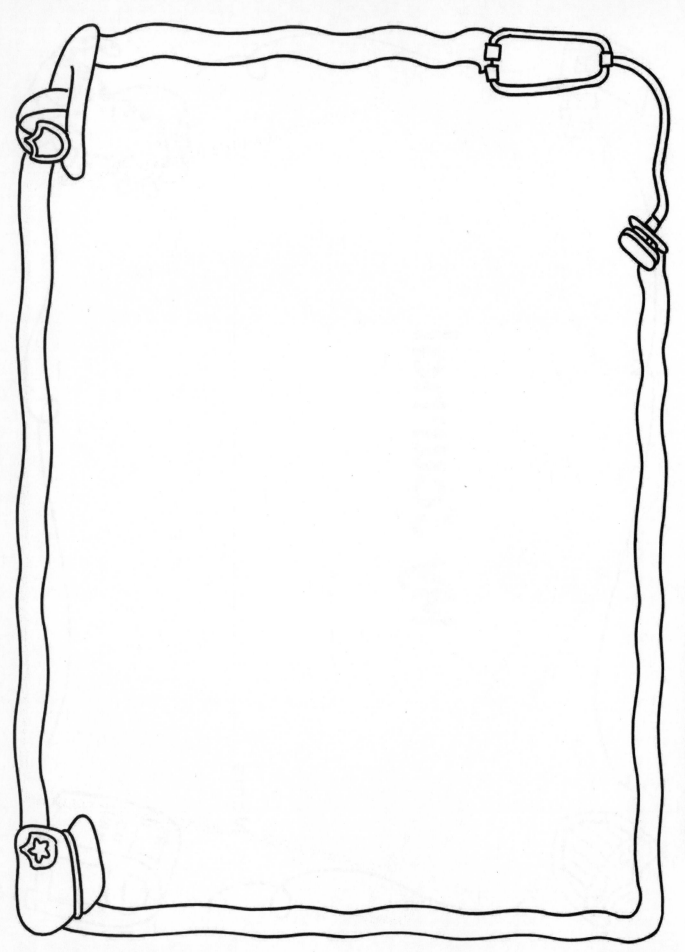

Border Paper

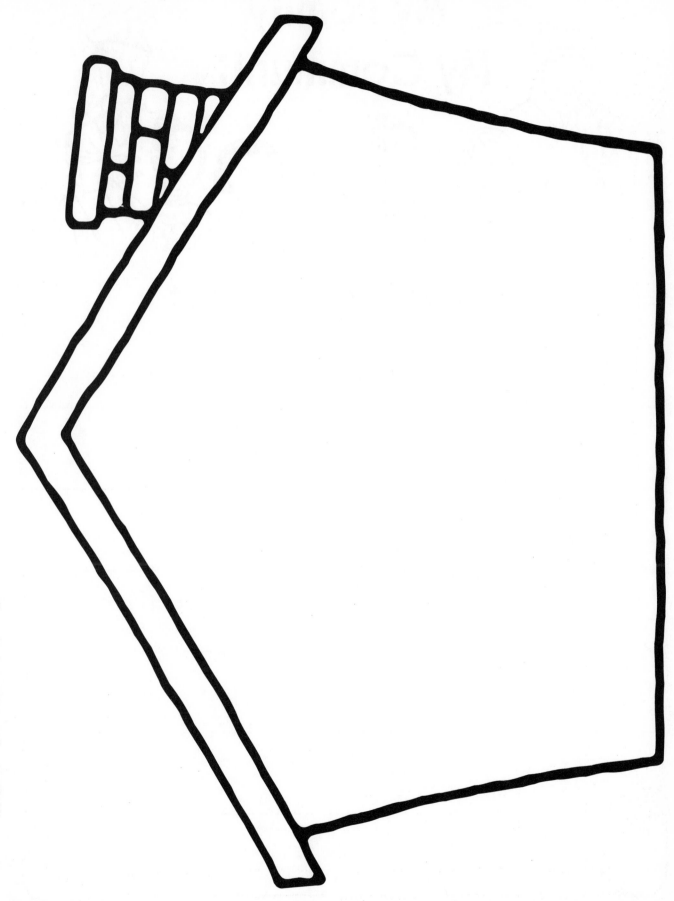

Shape Paper

My Family, My Community

Center Sign-Up Sheet

_____

_____

_____

_____

_____

_____

_____

Story Retelling Props for *Buzz*

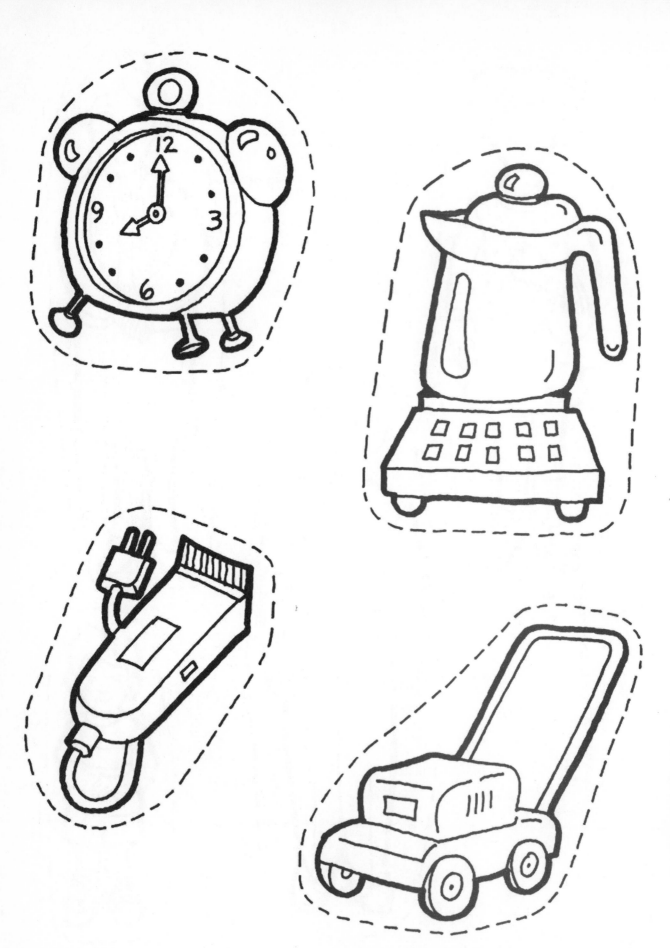

Story Retelling Props for *Buzz*

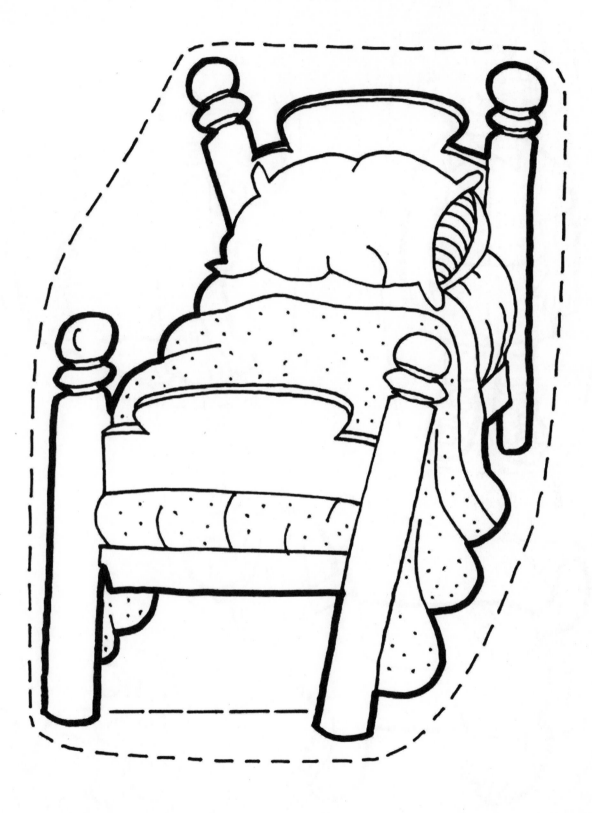

Story Retelling Props for "The Creaky Old Bed"

52   **THEME 2: My Family, My Community**

Story Retelling Props for "The Creaky Old Bed"

Story Retelling Props for *On Our Street*

Story Retelling Props for *On Our Street*

Story Retelling Props for "Too Much Noise"

Story Retelling Props for "Too Much Noise"

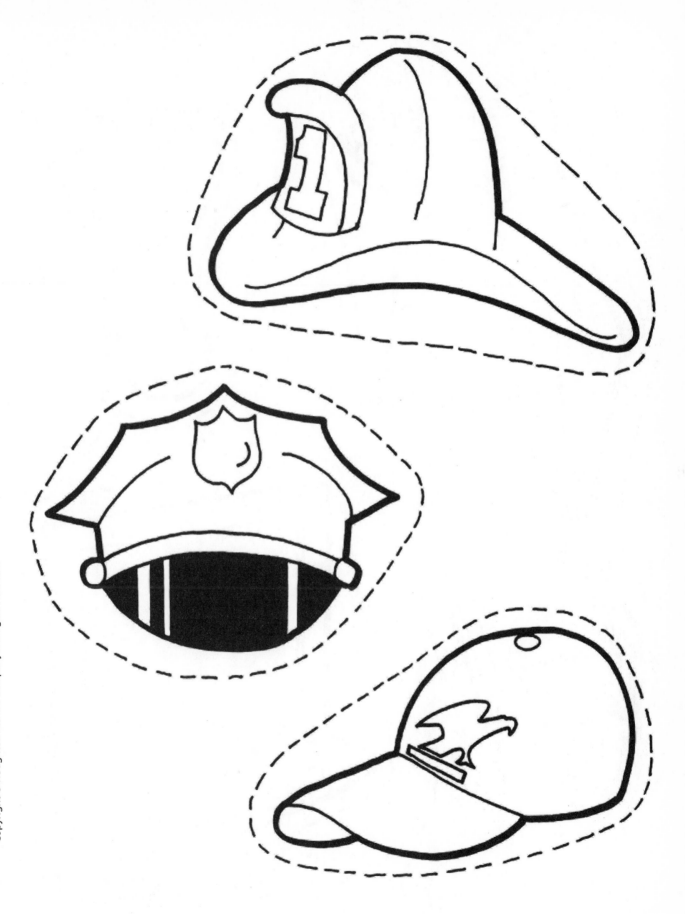

Story Retelling Props for *All Around Town*

Story Retelling Props for *All Around Town*

Story Retelling Props for "Stone Soup"

Story Retelling Props for "Stone Soup"

Families Together

Nancy Seaborn

Houghton Mifflin
PRE-K
Where Bright Futures Begin!

Theme 2: My Family, My Community

Think & Talk

What kinds of things do you do with your family?

ISBN 0-618513876

1-86111 LV PREK

9780618 513871

HOUGHTON MIFFLIN

Title Code: 1-86111

COVER Picturequest. **1** (l) Stockbyte/Getty Images. (r) Fat Chance Productions/Iconica.
2 (l) Johner/Photonica. (r) Jake Wyman/Photonica. **3** (l) SW Productions/Getty Images. (r) Mike
Brinson/The Image Bank/ Getty Images. **4** Davis Roth/Botanica/Getty Images. **5** Fat Chance
Productions/Iconica. **6** Picturequest. **7** Picturequest. **8** Picturequest.

Printed in Mexico by RR Donnelley

ISBN: 0-618-51387-6

Families Together

HOUGHTON MIFFLIN

Families have fun together!

8

Families do many things together.

2

We laugh.

7

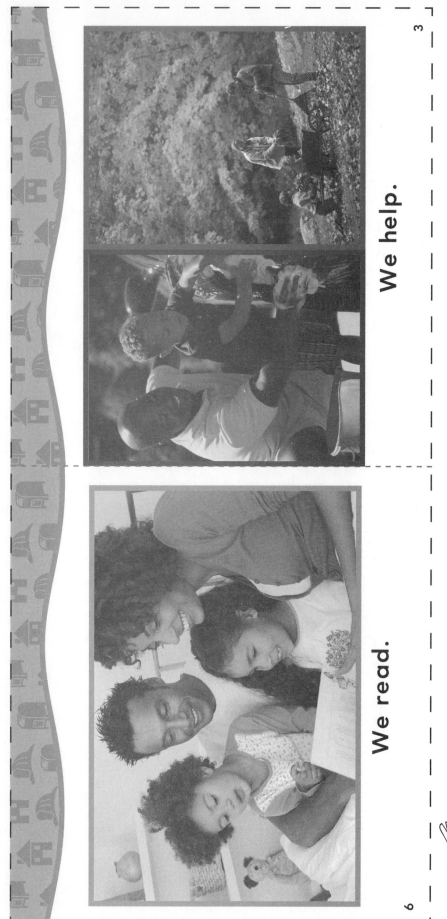

We help.

3

We read.

6

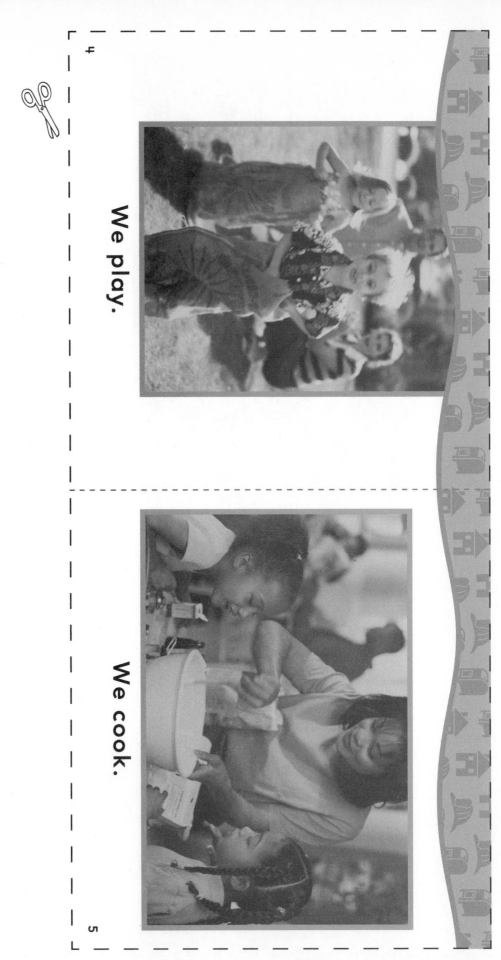

We play.

We cook.

4

5

Little Hands Library *Families Together*

apartment

baker

bus

car

dentist

doctor

family

firefighter

Picture-Word Cards

helmet

home

letter carrier

librarian

police officer

street

sidewalk

trash collector

Picture-Word Cards

My Five Senses

CONTENTS

Five Senses Just for Me!

lyrics by Jenny Reznick and Becky Manfredini
music by Harry Manfredini

Newsletter — WEEK 1 — My Five Senses

Dear Family,

This week _____ will learn about the five senses (hearing, sight, touch, taste, and smell). Using the topic "Using My Senses," we will read stories about how people use their senses. You can help your child learn more by talking with her/him about the things he/she is doing at school and the new letters and words that he/she is learning. Here are some ways that you can work with your child at home.

Think & Talk

What story did you read today?
What was the story about?
What parts of your body do you use to see? to touch?
What sounds do you hear in our kitchen? What do you smell?
What is your favorite thing to taste?

Home Activities

Small *t* Poster

Go on a small *t* hunt around your house. Find objects whose names begin with small *t* such as *telephone*, *table*, and *television*. Write and place labels on those objects.

Guessing Game

Play a senses guessing game with your child. For example, say *I hear a loud ringing sound.* Encourage your child to guess what you are describing. Take turns saying clues that begin *I hear* _____ , *I see* _____ , *I taste I feel* _____ , and *I smell* _____ .

What I Learned

Here is a note from your child and her/his teacher

Spanish Newsletter

My Five Senses

Querida familia:

Esta semana _____ va a aprender sobre los cinco sentidos (oído, vista, tacto, gusto y olfato). Usando el tema "Using My Senses" ("Usando mis sentidos"), leeremos cuentos sobre cómo la gente usa sus sentidos. Ustedes pueden ayudar a su niño o niña a aprender más hablándole sobre las cosas que está haciendo en la escuela y sobre las nuevas letras y palabras que está aprendiendo. A continuación hay algunas actividades que le pueden servir para trabajar con su hijo o hija en casa.

Pensar y conversar

¿Qué cuento leíste hoy? ¿Sobre qué se trataba el cuento?
¿Qué partes de tu cuerpo usas para (ver)?
¿Qué sonidos puedes escuchar en nuestra cocina?
¿Qué puedes oler?

Actividades para la casa

Afiche de la *t* minúscula

Busquen *t* minúsculas en su casa. Encuentren objetos cuyos nombres comienzan con *t* minúscula, como *teléfono, televisión* y *tina*. Escribe y pon letreros en estos objetos.

Juego de las adivinanzas

Jueguen a las adivinanzas con su hijo/a. Por ejemplo, digan *Oigo unas campanadas.* Anime a su hijo/a a adivinar de qué objeto se trata. Túrnense diciendo adivinanzas que comienzan con *Oigo* _____, *Huelo* _____, *Pruebo* _____, *Siento* _____, y *Veo* _____.

Lo que aprendí

Lean la nota que escribimos juntos.

Newsletter

My Five Senses

Dear Family,

This week _____ will learn about colors. Using the topic "Outside Our Door," we will be talking about the colors we see around us. You can help your child learn more by talking with her/him about the things he/she is doing at school and the new letters and words that he/she is learning. Here are some ways that you can work with your child at home.

Think & Talk

What did you read today?
What was the story about?
What colors did you learn about?
Where do you see your favorite color?

Home Activities

Collect Letters O and o

Look at magazine or newspaper headlines. Help your child find and cut out capital *O* and small *o*. Put the letters in an envelope or small box. Have your child count how many letter *O*s and *o*s they have in their collection. You can also sort the capital *O*s and small *o*s into two piles.

Reading Together

Children will listen to a book titled *Red Is a Dragon* this week. Read other books about colors with your child. Encourage her/him to talk about the illustrations.

What I Learned

Here is a note from your child and her/his teacher.

Spanish Newsletter

WEEK 2

My Five Senses

Querida familia:

Esta semana _____ va a aprender sobre los colores. Usando el tema "Outside Our Door" ("Afuera de nuestra puerta"), hablaremos sobre los colores que nos rodean. Ustedes pueden ayudar a su niño o niña a aprender más hablándole sobre las cosas que está haciendo en la escuela y sobre las nuevas letras y palabras que está aprendiendo. A continuación hay algunas actividades que le pueden servir para trabajar con su hijo o hija en casa.

Pensar y conversar

¿Qué leíste hoy?
¿Sobre qué se trataba el cuento?
¿Sobre qué colores aprendiste?
¿Dónde ves tu color favorito?

Actividades para la casa

Juntando letras *O* y *o*

Miren titulares de revistas y periódicos. Ayuden al niño/a a encontrar y recortar letras *O* mayúsculas y *o* minúsculas. Pongan las letras dentro de un sobre o una caja pequeña. Hagan que su niño/a cuente cuántas letras *O* y *o* tiene en su colección. También pueden clasificar las letras *O* mayúsculas y *o* minúsculas en dos grupos separados.

Leyendo juntos

Los niños escucharán el libro *Red Is a Dragon* esta semana. Lean con su hijo/a otros libros sobre colores. Anímenlo a hablar de las ilustraciones.

Lo que aprendí

Lean la nota que escribimos juntos.

Newsletter

WEEK 3

My Five Senses

Dear Family,

This week _____ will learn about patterns. Using the topic "We're Detectives!" we will read stories about patterns found in animals and objects. You can help your child learn more by talking with her/him about the things he/she is doing at school and the new letters and words that he/she is learning. Here are some ways that you can work with your child at home.

Think & Talk

What did you read today?
What was the story about?
What patterns did you learn about?
What patterns do you see around us?

Home Activities

Decorate *Xx*

Write a large capital *X* and small *x* on drawing paper. Spread glue on the letters and help your child decorate them with glitter, tissue paper, or another art material.

Animal Books

Children will listen to "How Cardinal Got His Red Feathers." Read other stories about animals with your child. Talk about how the animals in the stories are alike and different.

What I Learned

Here is a note from your child and her/his teacher.

Spanish Newsletter — WEEK 3 — My Five Senses

Querida familia:

Esta semana _____ va a aprender acerca de los diseños. Usando el tema "We're Detectives!" ("¡Somos detectives!"), leeremos cuentos sobre los diseños que se pueden encontrar en objetos y animales. Ustedes pueden ayudar a su niño o niña a aprender más hablándole sobre las cosas que está haciendo en la escuela y sobre las nuevas letras y palabras que está aprendiendo. A continuación hay algunas actividades que le pueden servir para trabajar con su hijo o hija en casa.

Pensar y conversar

¿Qué leíste hoy? ¿Sobre qué se trataba el cuento?
¿Qué diseños aprendiste hoy?
¿Qué diseños puedes ver a nuestro alrededor?

Actividades para la casa

Decorando Xx

Escriban una *X* mayúscula grande y una *x* minúscula pequeña en papel de dibujo. Apliquen pegamento y ayuden a su hijo/a a decorarlas con trocitos de papeles de colores u otros materiales de artes manuales.

Libros de animales

Los niños van a escuchar "How Cardinal Got His Red Feathers". Léanle otros cuentos sobre animales a su niño/a. Conversen sobre las diferencias y semejanzas que hay entre los animales de cada cuento.

Lo que aprendí

Lean la nota que escribimos juntos.

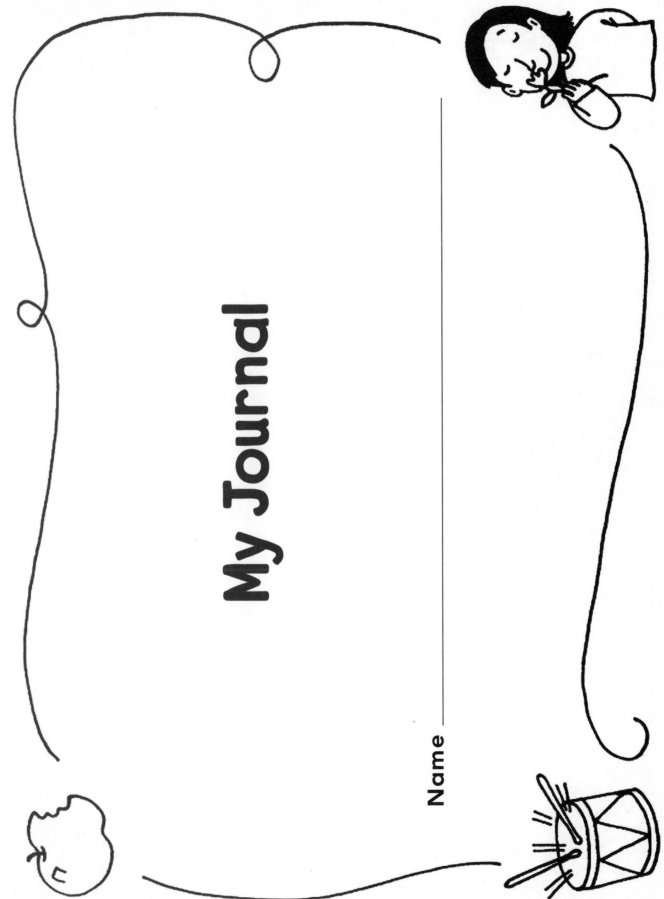

My Journal

Name _____

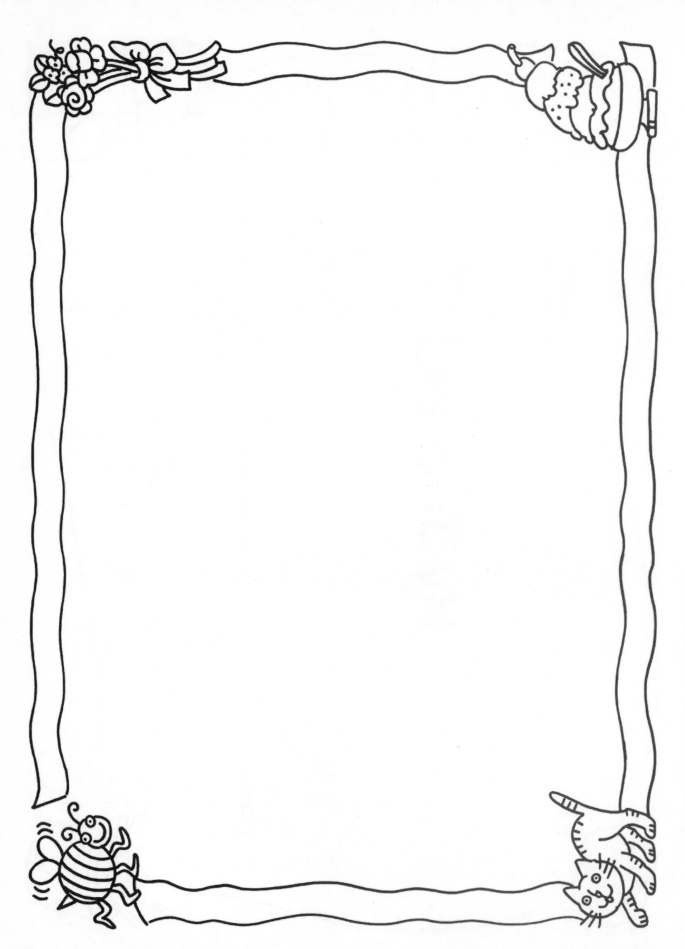

Border Paper

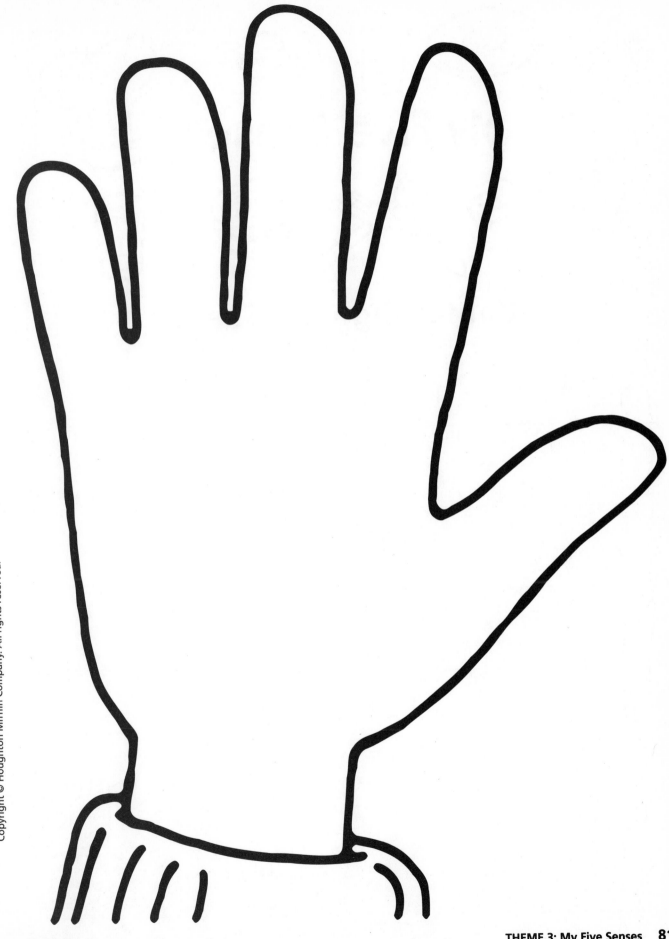

Shape Paper

My Five Senses

Center Sign-Up Sheet

Story Retelling Props for *The Body Book*

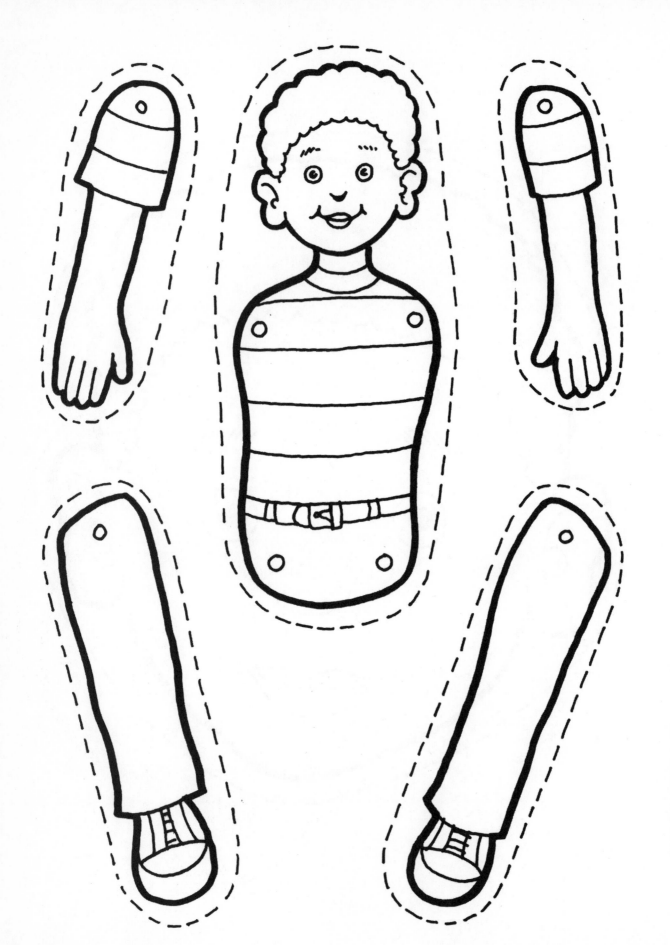

Story Retelling Props for *The Body Book*

Story Retelling Props for "Goldilocks and the Three Bears"

Story Retelling Props for "Goldilocks and the Three Bears"

Story Retelling Props for *Red is a Dragon*

Story Retelling Props for *Red is a Dragon*

Story Retelling Props for "How Cardinal Got His Red Feathers"

Story Retelling Props for "How Cardinal Got His Red Feathers"

Story Retelling Props for *Lots and Lots of Zebra Stripes*

Story Retelling Props for *Lots and Lots of Zebra Stripes*

Story Retelling Props for "How Zebra Got Its Stripes"

Story Retelling Props for "How Zebra Got Its Stripes"

FUN at the Park:

A Book About the Senses
Sean Trag

Houghton Mifflin
PRE-K
Where Bright Futures Begin!

Theme 3: My Five Senses

Think & Talk

What do you see, hear, smell, taste, and touch at a park?

ISBN 0-618513884
9 780618 513888
90000>
1-86112-LV PREK

HOUGHTON MIFFLIN

Title Code: 1-86112

COVER and 1 Martin Rogers/Getty Images. **2** Picturequest. **3** ElektraVision/Wonderfile. **4** Brian Smith. **5** Paula Hible/Getty Images. **6** Picturequest. **7** Tim Reese/Syracuse Newspapers/Image Works. **8** Picturequest. **9** Jake Wyman/Photonica.

Copyright (c) 2006 by Houghton Mifflin Company. All rights reserved.

No part of this work may be reproduced or transmitted in any form or by any means, electronic or mechanical, including photocopying or recording, or by any information storage or retrieval system without the prior written permission of Houghton Mifflin Company unless such copying is expressly permitted by federal copyright law. Address inquiries to School Permissions, Houghton Mifflin Company, 222 Berkeley Street, Boston, MA 02116.

Printed in Mexico by RR Donnelley

ISBN: 0-618-51388-4

Let's come back another day!

9

FUN at the Park:

A Book About the Senses

⚓ HOUGHTON MIFFLIN

The park is fun!

8

2

Let's go to the park!

Touch the water.

7

See the kites.

3

Taste the juice.

6

4

Hear the music.

Smell the popcorn.

5

Little Hands Library *Fun at the Park: A Book About the Senses*

eyes

ears

nose

mouth

hands

taste

hear

smell

Picture-Word Cards

touch

see

feathers

spots

tails

stripes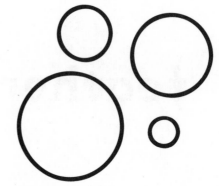

circles

triangles

Picture-Word Cards

squares

cube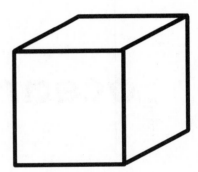

cone

cylinder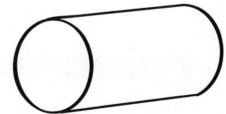

beach

ocean

sand

rainbow

Picture-Word Cards

Seasons All Around

CONTENTS

Summer, Fall, Winter, Spring

lyrics by Jenny Reznick and Becky Manfredini
music by Harry Manfredini

Gentle Waltz Tempo

Refrain

Verse 2

This season brings us morning dew
colored leaves and turkeys, too.
Orange pumpkins just for you!
We call this season fall.

Verse 3

This season brings us lots of snow
and happy songs that we all know.
Our cheeks turn red as cold winds blow.
We call this season winter.

Verse 4

This season brings us melted snow.
The plants and flowers start to grow.
Rainbows come and rainbows go.
We call this season Spring.

Theme Song

Newsletter — WEEK 1

Seasons All Around

Dear Family,

This week _____ will learn about the weather. Using the topic "Weather Report," we will read stories about how weather changes. You can help your child learn more by talking with her/him about the things he/she is doing at school and the new letters and words that he/she is learning. Here are some ways that you can work with your child at home.

Think & Talk

What kind of weather did you read about?
What do we like to do together on rainy days?
How about on sunny days?

Home Activities

Uu Umbrella

Cut out capital *U*s and small *u*s from newspaper and magazine headlines with your child. Draw an umbrella on a large piece of paper. Help your child glue the letters on the umbrella. Tell her/him that the word *umbrella* begins with *u*.

Stormy Weather

Your child will listen to a story titled "How Thunder and Lightning Came to Be." Ask him/her to talk about how he/she feels about thunder and lightning. Share books about thunder, lightning, or weather in general with your child.

What I Learned

Here is a note from your child and her/his teacher

Spanish Newsletter

WEEK 1

Seasons All Around

Querida familia:

Esta semana _____ va aprender sobre el clima. Usando el tema "Weather Report" ("El reporte del clima"), leeremos cuentos sobre cómo cambia el clima. Ustedes pueden ayudar a su niño o niña a aprender más hablándole sobre las cosas que está haciendo en la escuela y sobre las nuevas letras y palabras que está aprendiendo. A continuación hay algunas actividades que le pueden servir para trabajar con su hijo o hija en casa.

Pensar y conversar

¿Sobre qué tipos de clima leíste?
¿Qué nos gusta hacer en los días lluviosos?
¿Qué nos gusta hacer en los días soleados?

Actividades para la casa

El afiche de la *Uu*

Corten con su hijo/a letras *U* mayúsculas y *u* minúsculas de titulares de revistas y periódicos. Ayude a su hijo/a a pegar las letras en una hoja grande de papel. Pídanle que dibuje cosas que empiezan con *Uu,* como uvas y uñas.

Clima tormentoso

Su hijo va a escuchar un cuento titulado "How Thunder and Lighting Came to Be". Pídanle que hable de lo que siente cuando escucha truenos y ve rayos. Compartan con su niño/a libros sobre truenos y rayos, o sobre el clima en general.

Lo que aprendí

Lean la nota que escribimos juntos.

Newsletter — WEEK 2

Seasons All Around

Dear Family,

This week _____ will learn about nature. Using the topic "All Year Long," we will read stories about living things—animals and plants. You can help your child learn more by talking with her/him about the things he/she is doing at school and the new letters and words that he/she is learning. Here are some ways that you can work with your child at home.

Think & Talk

What do you like about the outdoors?
What plants do you see outside our house?
What animals do you see?

Home Activities

Yy Hunt

Look for words that begin with capital *Y* and small *y* in magazine and newspaper headlines. Circle the letters. Count the number of letters you find.

Books About Counting

Children will listen to a counting book titled *Swan Harbor* this week. Read other counting books with your child. Point out the numerals in the books. Count the items that correspond to each of the numerals.

What I Learned

Here is a note from your child and her/his teacher.

Spanish Newsletter

Seasons All Around

Querida familia:

Esta semana _____ va a aprender sobre la naturaleza. Usando el tema "All Year Long" ("A lo largo del año"), leeremos cuentos sobre los seres vivos—animales y plantas. Ustedes pueden ayudar a su niño o niña a aprender más hablándole sobre las cosas que está haciendo en la escuela y sobre las nuevas letras y palabras que está aprendiendo. A continuación hay algunas actividades que le pueden servir para trabajar con su hijo o hija en casa.

Pensar y conversar

¿Qué te gusta sobre el aire libre?
¿Qué plantas ves afuera de nuestra casa?
¿Qué animales ves?

Actividades para la casa

Buscando *Yy*

Busquen palabras que empiecen con *Y* mayúscula o *y* minúscula en titulares de periódicos y revistas. Encierren las letras en un círculo. Cuenten las letras que encontraron.

Libros de contar

Los niños van a escuchar un libro de contar titulado *Swan Harbor* esta semana. Lean con su hijo/a otros libros de contar. Señálenle los números en el libro. Cuenten los objetos que corresponden a cada número.

Lo que aprendí

Lean la nota que escribimos juntos.

Newsletter

Seasons All Around

Dear Family,

This week _____ will learn about the seasons. Using the topic "Seasons Change," we will read stories about how the weather changes throughout the year. You can help your child learn more by talking with her/him about the things he/she is doing at school and the new letters and words that he/she is learning. Here are some ways that you can work with your child at home.

Think & Talk

What did you read today?
What was the story about?
What season is it?
What is the weather like today?
What should we do today?

Home Activities

Ww Collage

Write *Ww* at the top of a large piece of paper. Help your child find pictures of objects whose names begin with *W* and *w* in newspapers, magazines, or catalogs. Make a collage with the pictures. You can also draw your own pictures.

Seasonal Books

Your child will listen to a book titled *What Makes the Seasons?* this week. Read other books about the seasons with your child. Talk about how the weather changes in each season.

What I Learned

Here is a note from your child and her/his teacher.

Spanish Newsletter

WEEK 3

Seasons All Around

Querida familia:

Esta semana _____ va a aprender a cerca de las estaciones. Usando el tema "Seasons Change" ("Las estaciones cambian"), leeremos cuentos sobre cómo cambia el clima a lo largo del año. Ustedes pueden ayudar a su niño o niña a aprender más hablándole sobre las cosas que está haciendo en la escuela y sobre las nuevas letras y palabras que está aprendiendo. A continuación hay algunas actividades que le pueden servir para trabajar con su hijo o hija en casa.

Pensar y conversar

¿Qué leíste hoy?
¿Sobre qué se trataba el cuento?
¿En qué estación estamos?
¿Cómo está el clima hoy? ¿Qué quieres hacer hoy?

Actividades para la casa

Collage con la *Ww*

Escriban *Ww* en la parte superior de una hoja grande de papel. Ayuden a su hijo/a a encontrar imágenes de objetos cuyos nombres empiezan con *W* y *w* en periódicos, revistas y catálogos. Hagan un *collage* con las imágenes. También pueden hacer sus propios dibujos.

Libros sobre las estaciones

Su hijo/a va a escuchar un libro titulado *What Makes the Seasons?* esta semana. Lean con su niño/a otros libros sobre las estaciones. Conversen sobre cómo cambia el clima en cada estación.

Lo que aprendí

Lean la nota que escribimos juntos.

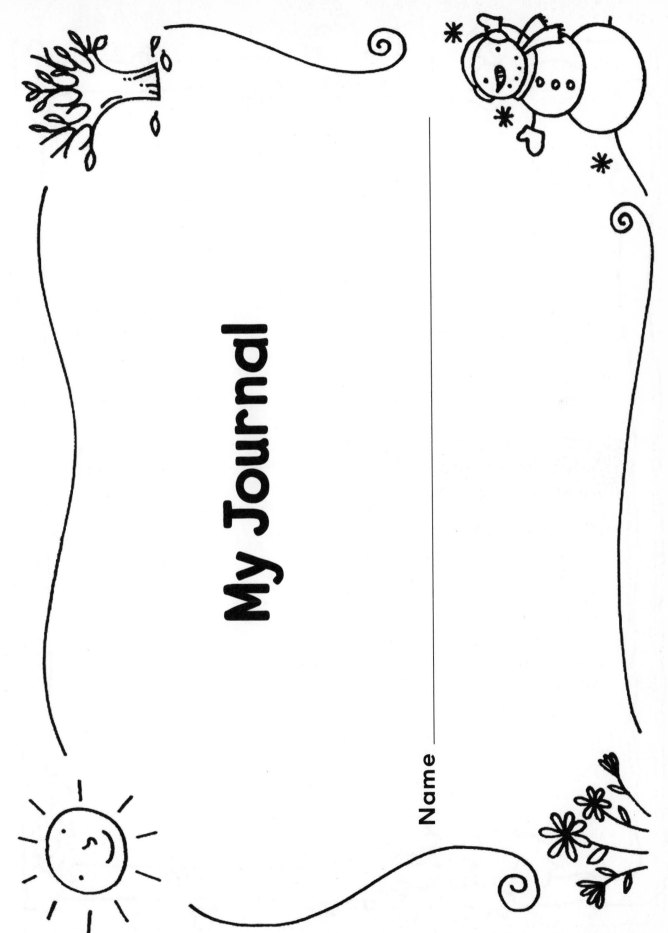

My Journal

Name _____

THEME 4: Seasons All Around

Border Paper

Shape Paper

Seasons All Around

Center Sign-Up Sheet

_____

_____

_____

_____

_____

_____

Story Retelling Props for *Bear in Sunshine*

Story Retelling Props for _Bear in Sunshine_

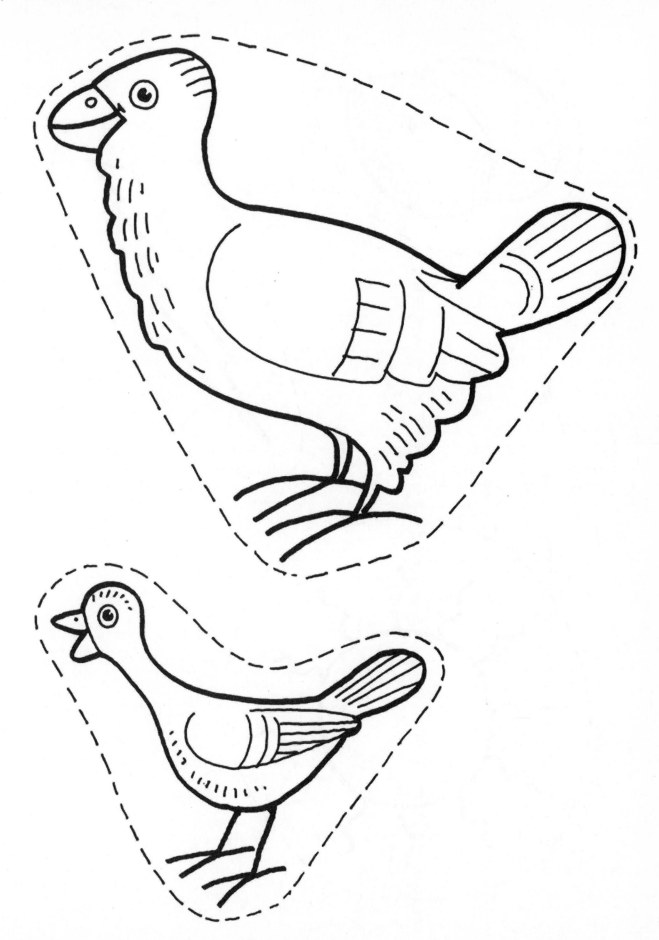

Story Retelling Props for "How Thunder and Lightning Came to Be"

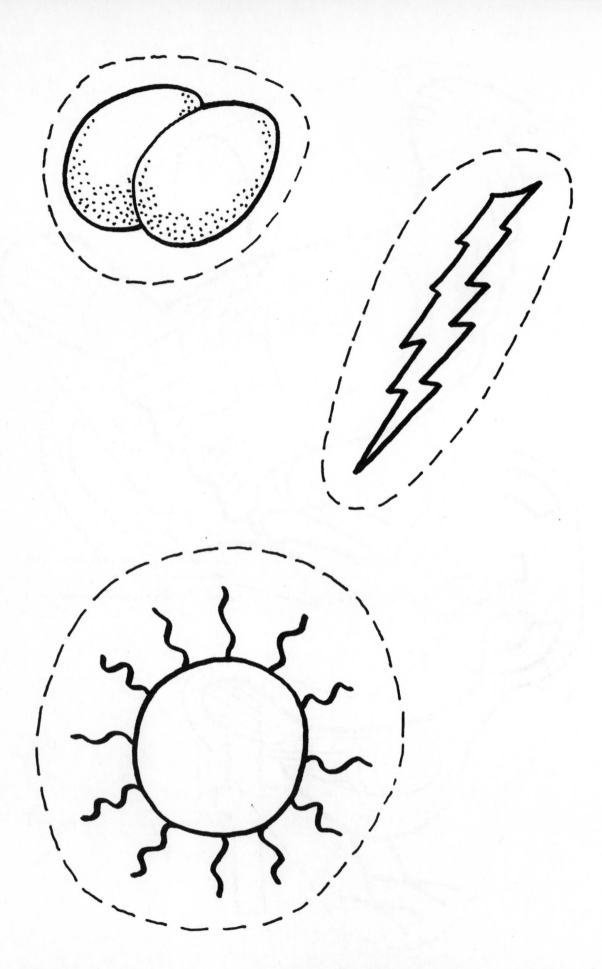

Story Retelling Props for "How Thunder and Lightning Came to Be"

Story Retelling Props for *Swan Harbor*

Story Retelling Props for *Swan Harbor*

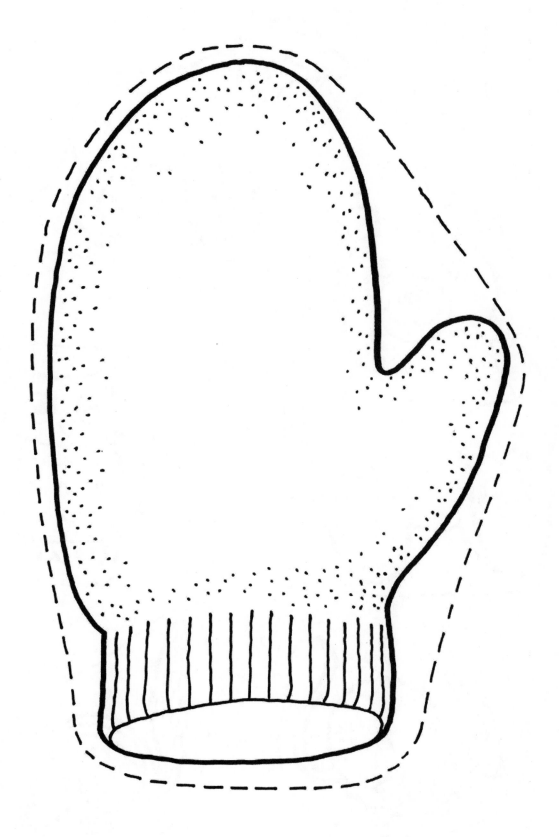

Story Retelling Props for "The Mitten"

Story Retelling Props for "The Mitten"

*Story Retelling Props for *What Makes the Seasons?**

Fall

Winter

Story Retelling Props for *What Makes the Seasons?*

Story Retelling Props for "The Grasshopper and the Ants"

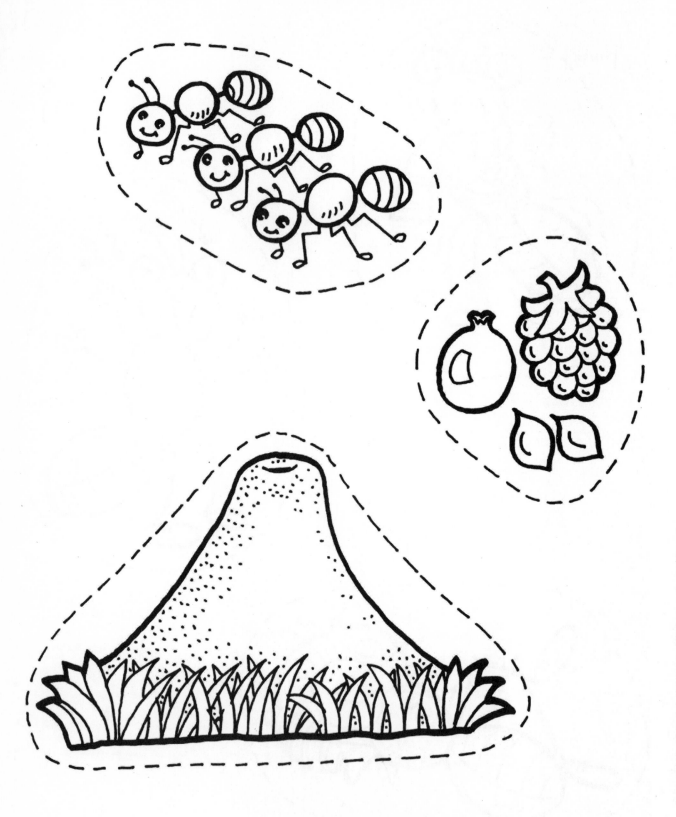

Story Retelling Props for "The Grasshopper and the Ants"

I Spy Seasons

Austin Hayes

Houghton Mifflin
PRE-K
Where Bright Futures Begin!

Theme 4: Seasons All Around

Think & Talk

What is your favorite season?

ISBN 0-618513892
90000>
9 780618 513895
1-86113-LV PREK

HOUGHTON MIFFLIN

Title Code: 1-86113

COVER (tr) Gerben Oppermans/Stone/Getty Images; (all other) PhotoDisc/Getty Images.
1 Gerben Oppermans/Stone/Getty Images; (all other) PhotoDisc/Getty Images. **2** (l,m) PhotoDisc/Getty Images; (r) Kathi Lamm/Stone/Getty Images. **3** (l,m) PhotoDisc/Getty Images; (r) Peter Beavis/Taxi/Getty Images. **4-5** (l) Nick Dolding/Stone/Getty Images; (m) PhotoDisc/Getty Images. **6** (l,m) PhotoDisc/Getty Images; (r) Augustus Buttera/Workbookstock; **7** (l,r) PhotoDisc/Getty Images; (m) Ewing Galloway/Index Stock. **8** (l) Tim Street Porter/Botanica/Getty Images; (b) Gary Buss/Taxi/Getty Images. **9** (l) Gerben Oppermans/ Stone/Getty Images; (m) Jeff/The Image Bank/Getty Images; (r) Miguel Salmeron/The Image Bank/Getty Images.

Copyright (c) 2006 by Houghton Mifflin Company. All rights reserved.
No part of this work may be reproduced or transmitted in any form or by any means, electronic or mechanical, including photocopying or recording, or by any information storage or retrieval system without the prior written permission of Houghton Mifflin Company unless such copying is expressly permitted by federal copyright law. Address inquiries to School Permissions, Houghton Mifflin Company, 222 Berkeley Street, Boston, MA 02116.
Printed in Mexico by RR Donnelley
ISBN: 0-618-51389-2

not belong in winter.

9

Little Hands Library *I Spy Seasons*

I Spy Seasons

Winter

Find something that does

8

2

Spring

Find something that does

not belong in fall.

7

Little Hands Library *I Spy Seasons*

Fall

Find something that does not belong in spring.

3

6

Summer

4

Find something that does

not belong in summer.

5

seasons

fall

spring

summer

winter

weather

wind

thunder

Picture-Word Cards

cloud

lightning

rain

snow

storm

sun

temperature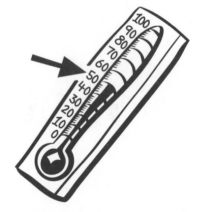

thermometer

Picture-Word Cards

calendar

date

mittens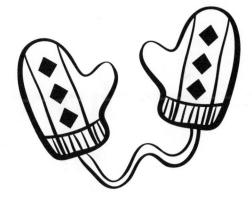

forest

year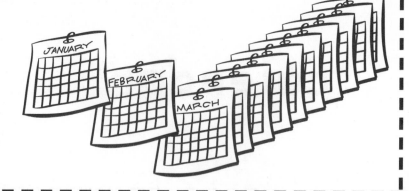

umbrella

orchard

Earth

Picture-Word Cards

Animals Everywhere

CONTENTS

I Love Animals!

lyrics by Jenny Reznick and Becky Manfredini
music by Harry Manfredini

Newsletter — WEEK 1

Animals Everywhere

Dear Family,

This week _____ will learn about pets. Using the topic "I Love Animals," we will read stories about pets and the experiences the pet owners have had with them. You can help your child learn more by talking with her/him about the things he/she is doing at school and the new letters and words that he/she is learning. Here are some ways that you can work with your child at home.

Think & Talk

What did you read today?
What was the story about?
What did you make today?
Do you think _____ would be/is a good pet for us? Why?

Home Activities

Ff Animal Poster

Draw a picture of a fish on a large piece of drawing paper. Tell your child that the word *fish* begins with the letter *f*. Children can decorate the poster by adding pictures of animals whose names begin with *f*, such as a frog or a fox.

Books About Pets

Your child will listen to the story "The Greedy Cat." Ask her/him to talk about how he/she feels about the cat that always wanted more. Read other books about pets with your child. Discuss what the pets in the stories are like.

What I Learned

Here is a note from your child and her/his teacher.

Spanish Newsletter

WEEK 1

Animals Everywhere

Querida familia:

Esta semana _____ va a aprender acerca de las mascotas. Usando el tema "I Love Animals" ("Amo a los animales"), leeremos cuentos sobre las mascotas y las experiencias que sus dueños tienen con ellas. Ustedes pueden ayudar a su niño o niña a aprender más hablándole sobre las cosas que está haciendo en la escuela y sobre las nuevas letras y palabras que está aprendiendo. A continuación hay algunas actividades que le pueden servir para trabajar con su hijo o hija en casa.

Pensar y conversar

¿Qué leíste hoy?
¿Sobre qué se trataba el cuento?
¿Qué hiciste hoy?
¿Crees que un/a _____ sería/es una buena mascota para nosotros? ¿Por qué?

Actividades para la casa

El afiche de animales de la *Ff*

Dibujen una foca en una hoja grande de papel. Díganle a su hijo o hija que la palabra *foca* comienza con *f* minúscula. Pueden decorar el afiche con fotografías o dibujos de animales cuyos nombres comiencen con *Ff*.

Libros sobre mascotas

Su hijo o hija escuchará un cuento titulado "The Greedy Cat". Pregúntenle cómo se siente que el gato siempre quiere más. Lean otros libros sobre mascotas son su hijo o hija. Conversen acerca de cómo son las mascotas de los cuentos.

Lo que aprendí

Lean la nota que escribimos juntos.

Newsletter

Animals Everywhere

Dear Family,

This week _____ will learn more about animals. Using the topic, "Animals We Know," we will read about the many different animals in our world. You can help your child learn more by talking with her/him about the things he/she is doing at school and the new letters and words that he/she is learning. Here are some ways that you can work with your child at home.

 Think & Talk

What animals did you read about today?
Which animal did you like the most? Why?
Do you think that animal would be a good pet?
Why or why not?

Home Activities

Aa Hunt

Look for words that begin with capital *A* and small *a* with your child in magazine and newspaper headlines. Circle and count the letters you find. Encourage your child to draw the letters on a blank piece of paper.

Counting Book

Your child will listen to the counting book *One Moose, Twenty Mice* this week. Ask her/him to tell about the animals in the book. Page through other counting books with your child. Encourage her/him to count the objects on each page and to predict what number will come next.

What I Learned

Here is a note from your child and her/his teacher.

Spanish Newsletter

Animals Everywhere

Querida familia:

Esta semana _____ va a aprender más sobre los animales. Usando el tema "Animals We Know" ("Animales que conocemos"), leeremos cuentos sobre la gran variedad de animales que hay en el mundo. Ustedes pueden ayudar a su niño o niña a aprender más hablándole sobre las cosas que está haciendo en la escuela y sobre las nuevas letras y palabras que está aprendiendo. A continuación hay algunas actividades que le pueden servir para trabajar con su hijo o hija en casa.

Pensar y conversar

¿Sobre qué animales leíste hoy?
¿Qué animal te gustó más? ¿Por qué?
¿Crees que ese animal sería una buena mascota?
¿Por qué sí o por qué no?

Actividades para la casa

Buscando *Aa*

Busquen con su hijo o hija palabras que empiecen con *A* mayúscula y *a* minúscula en titulares de periódicos y revistas. Encierren las letras en un círculo y cuéntenlas. Animen a su niño o niña a dibujar estas letras en una hoja de papel en blanco.

Libro de contar

Su hijo o hija escuchará esta semana el libro de contar *One Moose, Twenty Mice*. Pídanle sobre los animales. Hojeen otros libros de contar con su hijo o hija. Anímenlo/a a contar los objetos de cada página y a predecir que número vendrá después.

Lo que aprendí

Lean la nota
que escribimos juntos.

Newsletter — WEEK 3

Animals Everywhere

Dear Family,

This week _____ will learn more about animals. Using the topic "Animals on Land and Sea," we will read stories about animal families from around the world. You can help your child learn more by talking with her/him about the things he/she is doing at school and the new letters and words that he/she is learning. Here are some ways that you can work with your child at home.

Think & Talk

What animals did you read about today?
What did you learn about the animals?
What kind of animal home did you make?
How did you make it?

Home Activities

Zz Collage

Write *Zz* at the top of a large piece of paper. Help your child find *Zz* and pictures of objects whose names begin with *Zz* in magazines or catalogs. Glue them onto the paper. You can also draw your own pictures of *Zz* objects.

Animal Homes

Your child will listen to a story titled "Who's in Rabbit's House?" Ask her/him to tell you who was in Rabbit's house. Read other books about animals with your child. Point out and discuss the different places where the animals live.

What I Learned

Here is a note from your child and her/his teacher.

Animals Everywhere

Querida familia:

Esta semana _____ va a aprender más sobre los animales. Usando el tema "Animals on Land and Sea" ("Animales marinos y terrestres"), leeremos cuentos sobre familias de animales alrededor del mundo. Ustedes pueden ayudar a su niño o niña a aprender más hablándole sobre las cosas que está haciendo en la escuela y sobre las nuevas letras y palabras que está aprendiendo. A continuación hay algunas actividades que le pueden servir para trabajar con su hijo o hija en casa.

Pensar y conversar

¿Sobre qué animales leíste hoy?

¿Qué aprendiste sobre los animales?

¿Qué tipo de vivienda animal hiciste? ¿Cómo la hiciste?

Actividades para la casa

Afiche de *Zz*

Escriban *Zz* en la parte superior de una hoja grande de papel. Ayuden a su hijo o hija a encontrar en periódicos y revistas letras *Zz* e ilustraciones de objetos que empiecen por *Zz*. Péguenlos en la hoja de papel. Ustedes también pueden dibujar los objetos.

Viviendas de animales

Su hijo o hija escuchará el cuento "Who's in Rabbit's House?" Pídanle que les cuente quién estaba en la casa de Conejo. Lean otros libros sobre animales. Señalen y conversen sobre los lugares donde viven los animales.

Lo que aprendí

Lean la nota que escribimos juntos.

My Journal

Name _____

Border Paper

Shape Paper

Animals Everywhere
Center Sign-Up Sheet

Center Sign-Up Sheet

Story Retelling Props for *I Like Cats*

Story Retelling Props for *I Like Cats*

Story Retelling Props for "The Greedy Cat"

Story Retelling Props for "The Greedy Cat"

Story Retelling Props for *One Moose, Twenty Mice*

Story Retelling Props for "The Three Billy Goats Gruff"

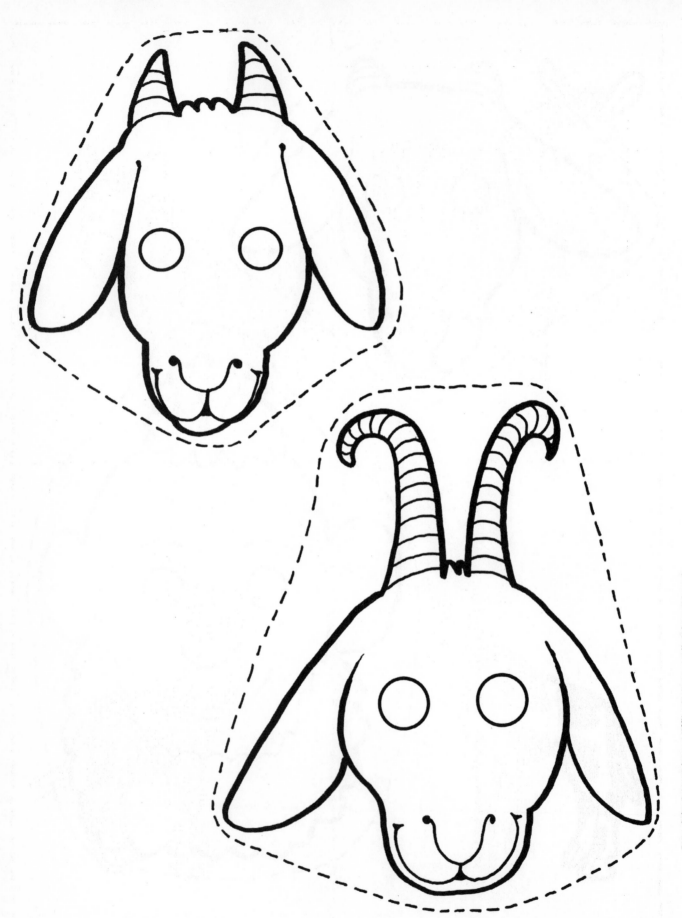

Story Retelling Props for "The Three Billy Goats Gruff"

Story Retelling Props for "Who's in Rabbit's House?"

Story Retelling Props for "Who's in Rabbit's House?"

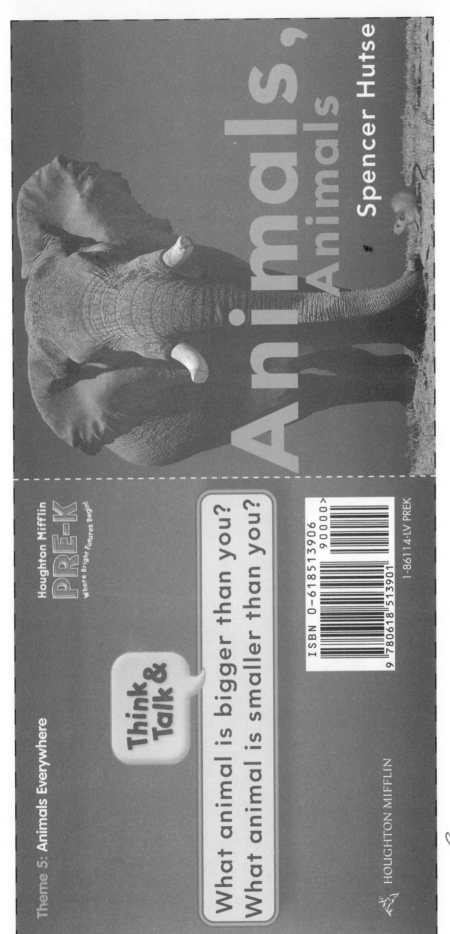

Animals, Animals

Spencer Hutse

Houghton Mifflin
PRE-K
Where Bright Futures Begin!

ISBN 0-618513906
90000>

9 780618 513901

1-86114-LV PREK

Theme 5: Animals Everywhere

Think & Talk

What animal is bigger than you?
What animal is smaller than you?

HOUGHTON MIFFLIN

Little Hands Library *Animals, Animals*

Title Code: 1-86114

COVER (l) Digital Vision/Getty Images; (r) PhotoDisc/Getty Images. **1** Digital Vision/Getty Images. **2** (l) Digital Vision/ Getty Images; (r) PhotoDisc/ Getty Images. **3** PhotoDisc/Getty Images. **4** (l) PhotoDisc/Getty Images; (r) Manoj Shah/Stone/Getty Images. **5** PhotoDisc/Getty Images. **6** (l) Artville; (r) PhotoDisc/Getty Images. **7** (t) PhotoDisc/Getty Images; (b) Artville. **8** (l) Steve Maslowski/Visuals Unlimited; (r) Mitsuaki Iwago/Minden Pictures. **9** (l) PhotoDisc/ Getty Images; (r) Corbis.

Copyright (c) 2006 by Houghton Mifflin Company. All rights reserved. No part of this work may be reproduced or transmitted in any form or by any means, electronic or mechanical, including photocopying or recording, or by any information storage or retrieval system without the prior written permission of Houghton Mifflin Company unless such copying is expressly permitted by federal copyright law. Address inquiries to School Permissions, Houghton Mifflin Company, 222 Berkeley Street, Boston, MA 02116.

Printed in Mexico by RR Donnelley

ISBN: 0-618-51390-6

Who is louder?

9

Little Hands Library *Animals, Animals*

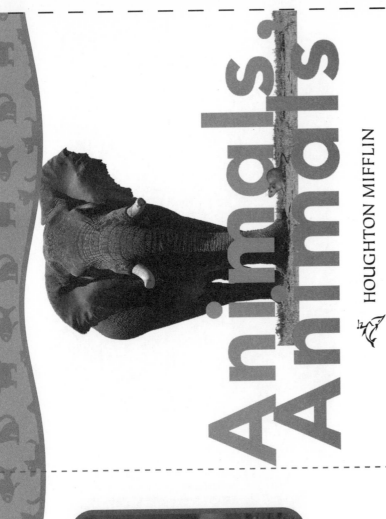

Animals, Animals

HOUGHTON MIFFLIN

Who is heavier?

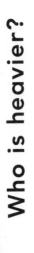

8

Who is bigger?

2

Who is slower?

7

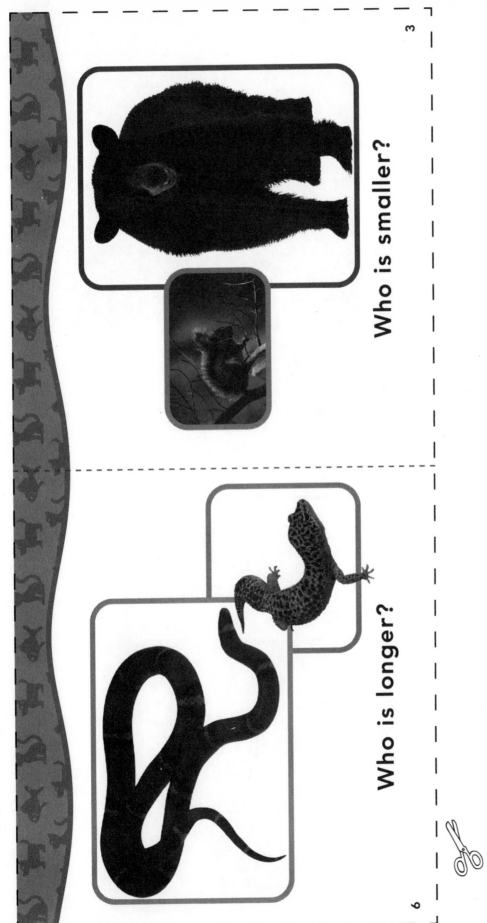

Who is smaller?

3

Who is longer?

6

Little Hands Library *Animals, Animals*

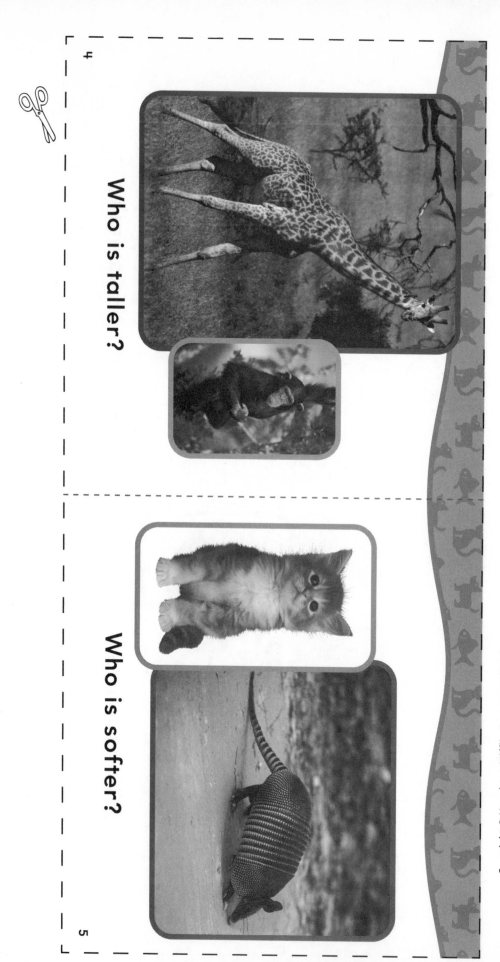

Who is taller?

Who is softer?

4

5

animals

babies

barn

bear

bird

cats

clock

desert

Picture-Word Cards

dog

elephant

farm

fish

goats

cave

mice

moose

Picture-Word Cards

park

penguin

zoo

pet

pond

rabbit

tank

zebra

Picture-Word Cards

Construction Zone

CONTENTS

The Construction Zone

lyrics by Jenny Reznick and Becky Manfredini
music by Harry Manfredini

Easy Rock Tempo

Theme Song

Newsletter

Construction Zone

Dear Family,

This week _____ will learn about building things. Using the topic "I Can Build," we will read stories about tools, materials, buildings, and construction. You can help your child learn more by talking with her/him about things he/she is doing at school and the new letters and words that he/she is learning. Here are some ways that you can work with your child at home.

Think & Talk

What did you read today?
What was your favorite part of the story?
What did you build today?
What would you like to build tomorrow?

Home Activities

Bb Poster

Gather *Bb*s from newspaper or magazine headlines. Help your child make a *Bb* poster. You can decorate the poster by adding pictures or photographs of things whose names start with *Bb*.

Learning the ABCs

Your child will listen to the alphabet book *Alphabet Under Construction* this week. Page through other alphabet books together, paying special attention to the *ABC* order. Encourage your child to predict what letter you will read about next in the book.

What I Learned

Here is a note from your child and her/his teacher.

Spanish Newsletter — WEEK 1 — Construction Zone

Querida familia:

Esta semana _____ va a aprender sobre la construcción. Usando el tema "I Can Build" ("Yo puedo construir"), leeremos cuentos sobre herramientas, materiales y construcciones. Ustedes pueden ayudar a su niño o niña a aprender más hablándole sobre las cosas que está haciendo en la escuela y sobre las nuevas letras y palabras que está aprendiendo. A continuación hay algunas actividades que le pueden servir para trabajar con su hijo o hija.

Pensar y conversar

¿Qué leíste hoy?

¿Sobre qué se trata el cuento?

¿Cuál es tu parte favorita del cuento?

¿Qué construiste hoy? ¿Qué materiales usaste?

¿Qué te gustaría construir mañana?

Actividades para la casa

El afiche de la *Bb*

Recorten letras *Bb* de los titulares de periódicos o revistas. Ayude a su hijo o hija a hacer un afiche de la *Bb*. Pueden decorar el afiche con dibujos o fotografías de objetos cuyos nombres empiezan con *Bb*.

Aprendiendo el *ABC*

Esta semana su hijo o hija escuchará el libro de alfabeto *Alphabet Under Construction*. Hojeen juntos otros libros similares, poniendo especial atención al orden alfabético. Anime a su hijo o hija a que prediga cuál es la letra que usted le leerá.

Lo que aprendí

Lean la nota que escribimos juntos.

Newsletter

Construction Zone

Dear Family,

This week _____ will learn about solving problems. Using the topic "Build with Me," we will read stories about building things and working together to solve problems. You can help your child learn more by talking with her/him about things he/she is doing at school and the new letters and words that he/she is learning. Here are some ways that you can work with your child at home.

Think & Talk

What did you read today?
What was the problem in the story?
How was it solved?
What problem did you solve today?

Home Activities

Mm Hunt

Look for *Mm*s in newspaper and magazine headlines. Underline the *Mm*s you find and count them together. Encourage your child to trace the letters so he/she can familiarize herself/himself with their shape.

Building Bugs

Your child will listen to the book *Bumbling Building Bugs* this week. It is about a group of bugs that work together to build a road and a bridge. Ask your child to tell you about the different bugs in the book. Observe harmless insects outside.

What I Learned

Here is a note from your child and her/his teacher.

Spanish Newsletter — WEEK 2

Construction Zone

Querida familia:

Esta semana _____ va a aprender acerca de resolver problemas. Usando el tema "Build with Me" ("Construye conmigo"), leeremos cuentos sobre el trabajo en grupo para resolver problemas. Ustedes pueden ayudar a su niño o niña a aprender más hablándole sobre las cosas que está haciendo en la escuela y sobre las nuevas letras y palabras que está aprendiendo. A continuación hay algunas actividades que le pueden servir para trabajar con su hijo o hija en casa.

Pensar y conversar

¿Qué leíste hoy?
¿Cuál es el problema en el cuento?
¿Cómo se resuelve el problema?

Actividades para la casa

Buscando *Mm*

Busquen *Mm* en los titulares de periódicos o revistas. Subrayen las letras *Mm* que encuentren. Cuéntenlas juntos. Animen a su niño o niña a trazar las letras para que se familiarice con su forma.

Insectos constructores

Su hijo o hija escuchará esta semana el libro *Bumbling Building Bugs*. Es sobre un grupo de insectos que trabajan juntos en la construcción de un camino y un puente. Pidan a su hijo o hija que les cuente sobre los diferentes insectos en el libro. Observen insectos afuera.

Lo que aprendí

Lean la nota que escribimos juntos.

Newsletter — WEEK 3

Construction Zone

Dear Family,

This week _____ will learn about how children can plan together to get a job done. Using the topic "Everybody Builds," we will read stories about how building things requires planning and working together. You can help your child learn more by talking with her/him about the things he/she is learning at school and the new letters and words that he/she is learning. Here are some ways that you can work with your child at home.

Think & Talk

What did you read today?
What was the story about?
What did the characters build?
How did they work together to get things done?

Home Activities

Looking for *Rr*

Look for *Rr*s on food packaging, such as cereal boxes and labels on cans. You can also look for *Rr*s on signs around your neighborhood. Encourage your child to tell you whether the letter is capital *R* or small *r*.

Reading Together

Your child will listen to the classic folktale "The Three Little Pigs" this week. Read other versions of this story with your child. Talk about how the stories are alike and different.

What I Learned

Here is a note from your child and her/his teacher.

Spanish Newsletter

WEEK 3

Construction Zone

Querida familia:

Esta semana _____ va aprender cómo los niños pueden hacer planes en grupo para hacer un trabajo. Usando el tema "Everybody Builds" ("Todos construimos"), leeremos cuentos sobre cómo la construcción requiere de planeación y trabajo en grupo. Ustedes pueden ayudar a su niño o niña a aprender más hablándole sobre las cosas que está haciendo en la escuela y sobre las nuevas letras y palabras que está aprendiendo. A continuación hay algunas actividades que le pueden servir para trabajar con su hijo o hija.

Pensar y conversar

¿Qué leíste hoy?

¿Sobre qué se trata el cuento?

¿Qué construyen los personajes?

¿Cómo trabajan juntos para lograr hacer las cosas?

Actividades para la casa

Buscando *Rr*

Busquen las letras *Rr* en empaques de comida, como cajas de cereal o latas. También pueden buscar *Rr* en señales de tránsito de su vecindario. Animen a su niño o niña a decir si la letra es una *R* mayúscula o una *r* minúscula.

Leyendo juntos

Su hijo o hija escuchará esta semana el cuento popular "The Three Little Pigs". Lean otras versiones de la historia con su niño o niña. Conversen sobre las diferencias y semejanzas en las historias.

Lo que aprendí

Lean la nota que escribimos juntos.

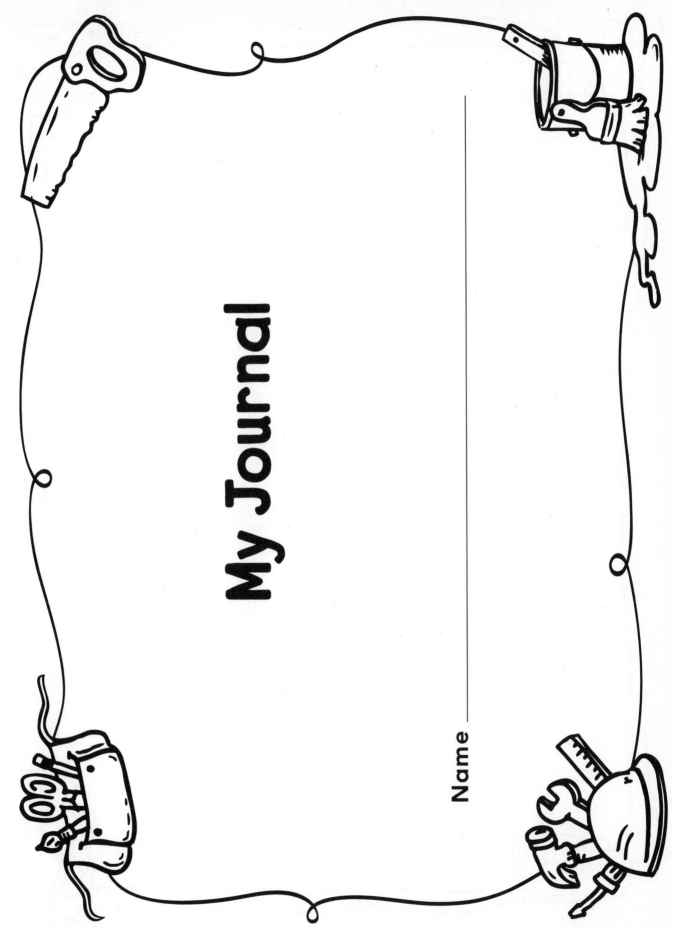

My Journal

Name _____

Journal Cover

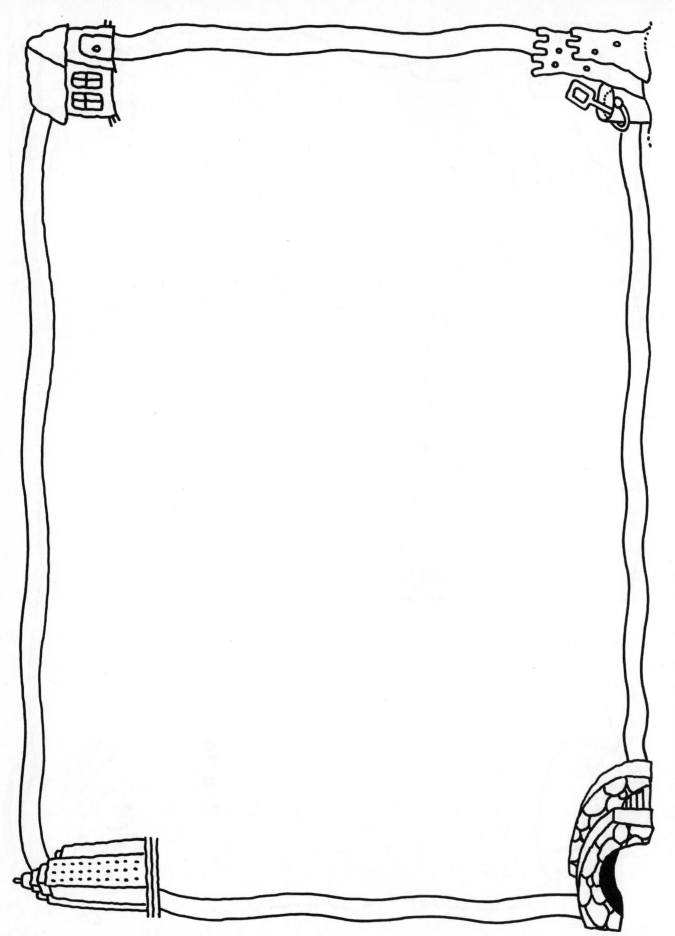

Border Paper

Shape Paper

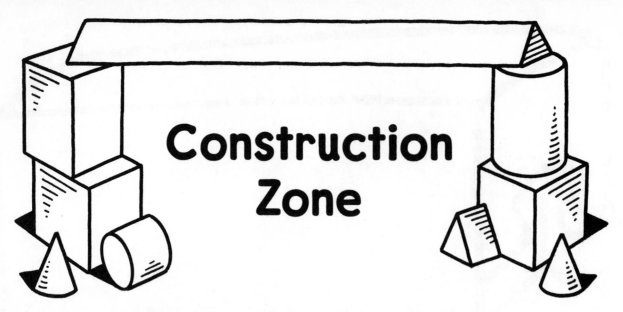

Construction Zone

Center Sign-Up Sheet

_____

_____

_____

_____

_____

_____

Center Sign-Up Sheet

Story Retelling Props for *Alphabet Under Construction*

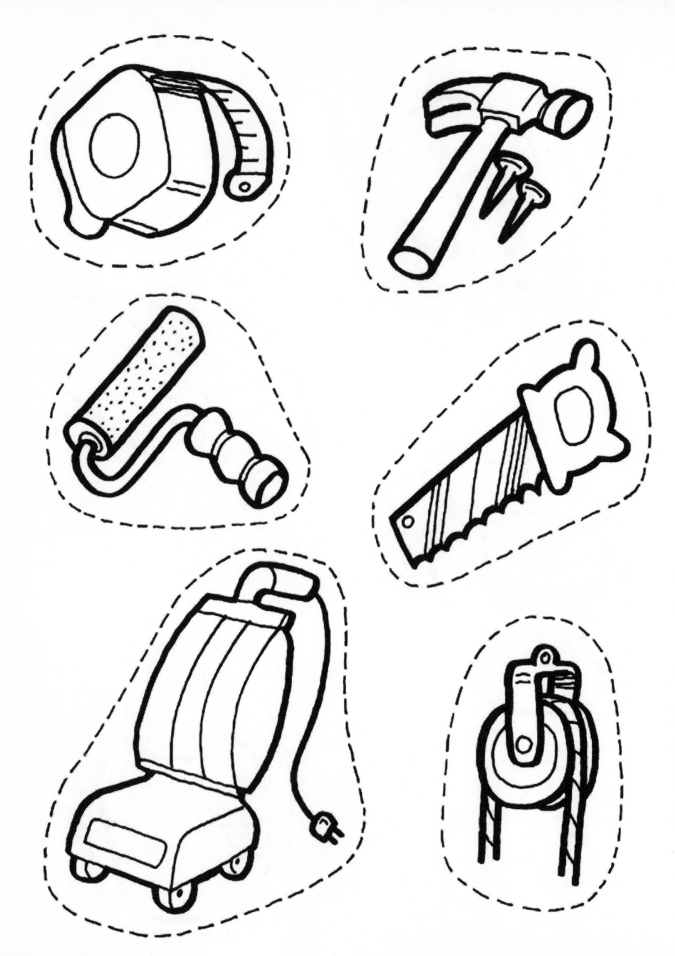

Story Retelling Props for *Alphabet Under Construction*

Story Retelling Props for "The Elves and the Shoemaker"

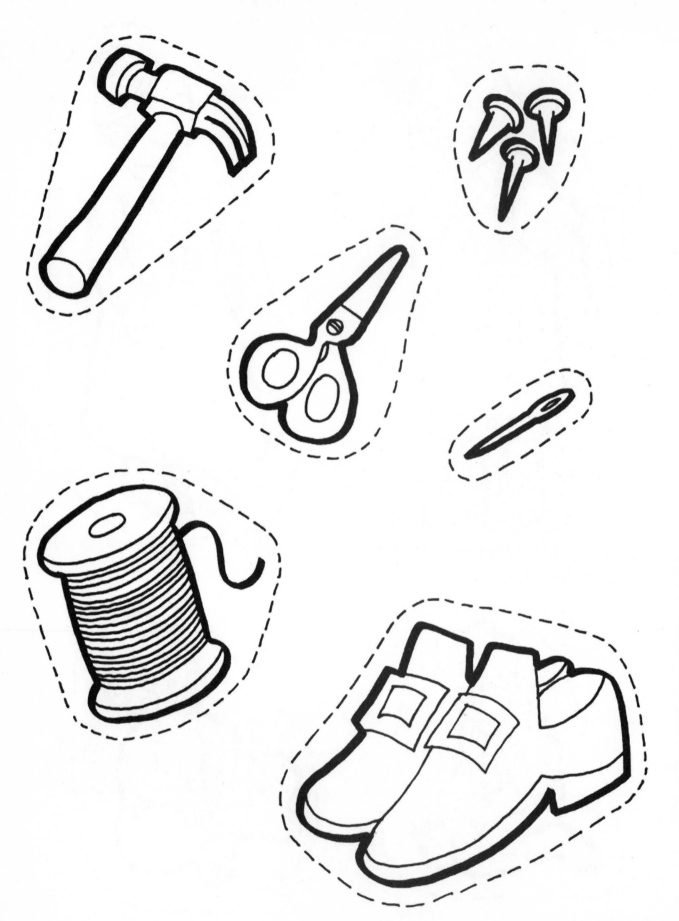

THEME 6: Construction Zone

Story Retelling Props for "The Elves and the Shoemaker"

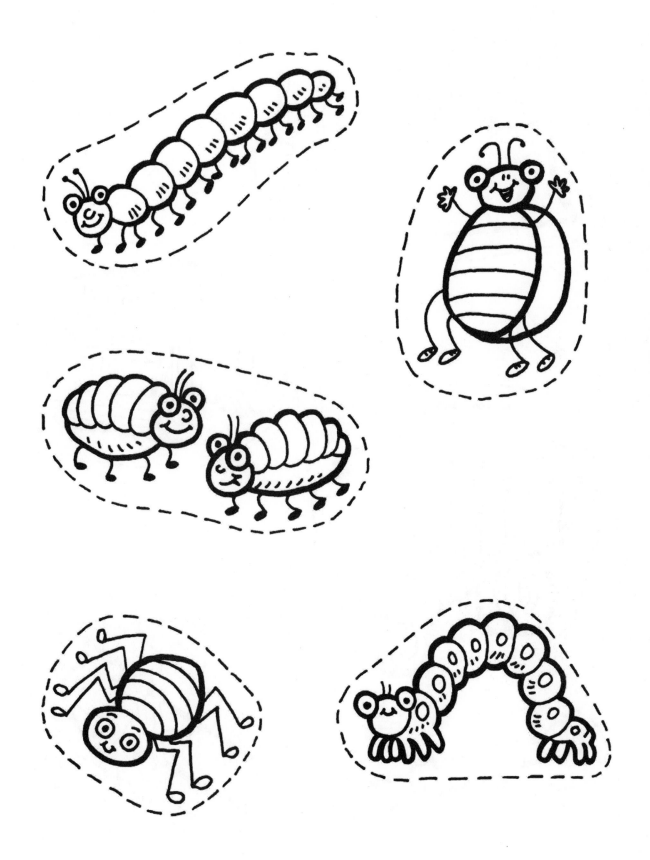

Story Retelling Props for *Bumbling Building Bugs*

Story Retelling Props for *Bumbling Building Bugs*

Story Retelling Props for "The Builder and the Oni"

Story Retelling Props for "The Builder and the Oni"

Story Retelling Props for *Raise the Roof!*

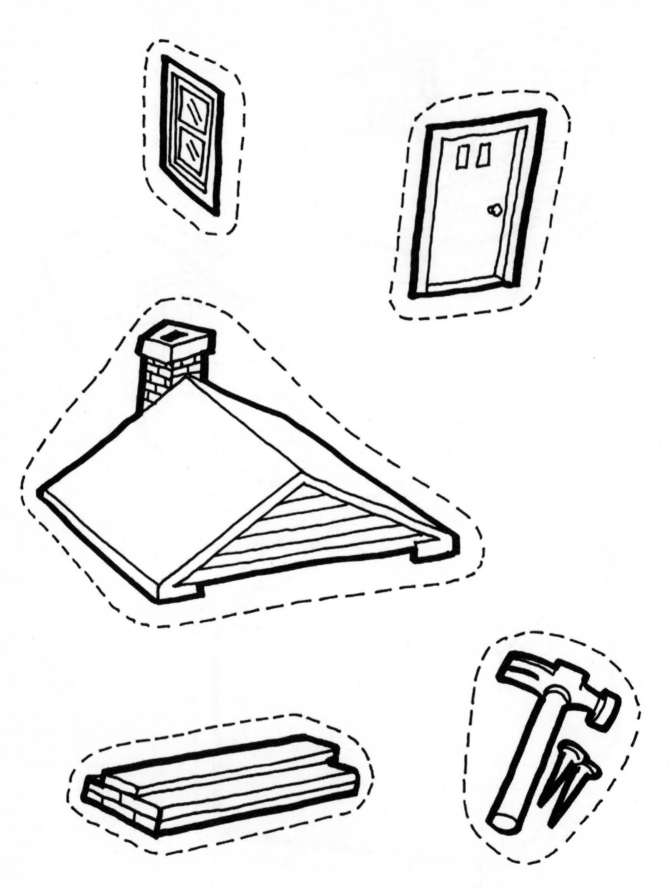

Story Retelling Props for *Raise the Roof!*

Story Retelling Props for "The Three Little Pigs"

Story Retelling Props for "The Three Little Pigs"

I Build, Too!

John Connor

Think & Talk

What can you build?

Title Code: 1-86115

COVER Cheryl Clegg. 1 Thinkstock/Getty Images. 2 Vince Streano/The Image Works. 3 Felicia Martinez/PhotoEdit. 4 Tony Freeman/PhotoEdit 5 Gary Waltz/The Image Works. 6 Mitch Kezar/Stone/Getty images. 7 Tony Freeman/PhotoEdit. 8 (l) David Joel/Stone/Getty Images. (r) Lester Lefkowitz/The Images Bank/Getty Images. 9 (l) Ellen B. Senisi/The Image Works. (r) Jeff Greenberg/PhotoEdit.

Printed in Mexico by RR Donnelley
ISBN: 0-618-51391-4

I build whole cities, too!

9

I Build, Too!

HOUGHTON MIFFLIN

BOSTON

Some people build whole cities!

8

Some people build houses.

2

I build towers, too.

7

I build houses, too.

3

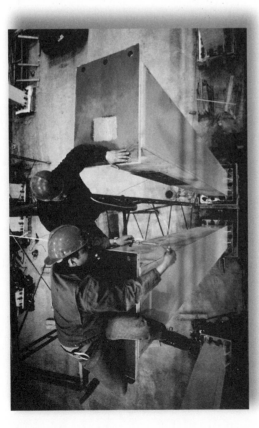

Some people build towers.

6

4

Some people build roads.

I build roads, too.

5

Little Hands Library *I Build, Too!*

build

machine

tools

blocks

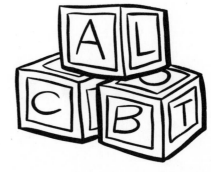

building

road

hammer

scissors

Picture-Word Cards

needle

saws

bridge

stream

hangs

rolls

repair

house

Picture-Word Cards

tattered

glues

roof

cuts

under
construction

unroll

ices

make

In the City, In the Country

CONTENTS

The City and the Country

lyrics by Jenny Reznick and Becky Manfredini
music by Harry Manfredini

Newsletter

In the City, In the Country

Dear Family,

This week _____ will learn about the country. Using the topic "Country Life," we will read stories about rural areas and farms, and what it is like to live there. You can help your child learn more by talking with her/him about the things he/she is doing at school and the new letters and words that he/she is learning. Here are some ways that you can work with your child at home.

Think & Talk

What kinds of animals live on farms?
What sounds do these animals make?
Why do you like (horses) so much?

Home Activities

Country Poster

Collect *Cc* from newspaper and magazine headlines with your child. Write *Country* on drawing paper. Find pictures of farm animals whose names begin with *c*, such as cows. Help your child glue the animal pictures and letters *Cc* on the drawing paper to make a poster.

Country Books

Your child will listen to a story titled "The Billy Goat in the Garden." Ask him/her to tell about the naughty billy goat. Read other books about farm animals with your child.

What I Learned

Here is a note from your child and her/his teacher.

Spanish Newsletter

In the City, In the Country

Querida familia:

Esta semana _____ va a aprender sobre el campo. Usando tema "Country Life" ("Vida en el campo"), leeremos cuentos sobre las áreas rurales y las granjas, y sobre la vida en ellas. Ustedes pueden ayudar a su niño o niña a aprender más hablándole sobre las cosas que está haciendo en la escuela y sobre las nuevas letras y palabras que está aprendiendo. A continuación hay algunas actividades que le pueden servir para trabajar con su hijo o hija en casa.

Pensar y conversar

¿Qué tipo de animales viven en las granjas?
¿Qué sonidos hacen estos animales?
¿Por qué te gustan tanto (los caballos)?

Actividades para la casa

Afiche campestre

Reúnan *Cc* de los titulares de periódicos y revistas con su hijo/a. Escriban *El campo* en una hoja de papel de dibujo. Encuentren imágenes de animales cuyos nombres empiezan por *c*, como *caballo.* Ayuden a su niño/a a pegar las imágenes de animales y las letras.

Libros sobre el campo

Su hijo/a va escuchar el cuento "The Billy Goat in the Garden". Pídanle que les hable de la traviesa cabra. Lean con él/ella otros libros sobre animales de granja.

Lo que aprendí

Lean la nota que escribimos juntos.

Newsletter — WEEK 2

In the City, In the Country

Dear Family,

This week _____ will learn about the city. Using the topic "The Busy, Busy City," we will read stories about what it is like to live in the city and how people get around there. You can help your child learn more by talking with her/him about the things he/she is doing at school and the new letters and words that he/she is learning. Here are some ways that you can work with your child at home.

Think & Talk

What did you learn about the city today?
What do you think it is like to ride in a subway?
What other ways do people get around in a city?

Home Activities

Qq Hunt

Look at magazine and newspaper headlines with your child. Circle the words that begin with capital *Q* and small *q*. Count the number of letters you find.

City Books

Children will listen to a story titled "City Mouse and Country Mouse" this week. Ask your child to tell what happens when the country mouse visits the city. Read other books about the city with your child. Discuss what your child sees in the illustrations.

What I Learned

Here is a note from your child and her/his teacher.

Spanish Newsletter

In the City, In the Country

Querida familia:

Esta semana _____ va a aprender sobre la ciudad. Usando el tema "The Busy, Busy City" ("La agitada ciudad"), leeremos cuentos sobre cómo es vivir en la ciudad y las formas como las personas viajan por ella. Ustedes pueden ayudar a su niño o niña a aprender más hablándole sobre las cosas que está haciendo en la escuela y sobre las nuevas letras y palabras que está aprendiendo. A continuación hay algunas actividades que le pueden servir para trabajar con su hijo o hija en casa.

Pensar y conversar

¿Qué aprendiste hoy sobre la ciudad?

¿Cómo crees que es viajar en metro?

¿De qué otras maneras se mueven las personas por la ciudad?

Actividades para la casa

Buscando *Qq*

Vean con su hijo o hija los titulares de revistas y periódicos. Encierren con círculos las palabras que comienzan con *Q* mayúscula o *q* minúscula. Cuenten el número de letras que encuentren.

Libros sobre la ciudad

Los niños o niñas van a escuchar esta semana un cuento titulado "City Mouse and Country Mouse". Pídanle que les cuente lo que pasa cuando el ratón del campo visita la ciudad. Lean otros libros sobre la ciudad con su hijo o hija. Conversen sobre lo que ven en las ilustraciones.

Lo que aprendí

Lean la nota que escribimos juntos.

Newsletter — WEEK 3

In the City, In the Country

Dear Family,

This week _____ will learn about buying and selling things. Using the topic "To Market, To Market," we will talk about the different things people buy and sell. You can help your child learn more by talking with her/him about the things he/she is doing at school and the new letters and words that he/she is learning. Here are some ways that you can work with your child at home.

Think & Talk

What did you read today?
What was the story about?
What can you make with apples?
What can you do with the things you make?

Home Activities

Vv Van

Draw the outline of a van on a piece of paper. Help your child find *Vv*s in magazine and newspaper headlines. Circle the letters and cut them out. Help your child paste the letters on the van.

Reading Together

Children will listen to a story titled "The Apple Dumpling." Ask your child to name things the old woman in the story trades to get apples to make the dumpling. Read other stories about buying and selling things with your child.

What I Learned

Here is a note from your child and her/his teacher.

In the City, In the Country

Querida familia:

Esta semana _____ va a aprender sobre comprar y vender cosas. Usando el tema "To Market, To Market" ("Al mercado"), conversaremos sobre las diferentes cosas que las personas compran y venden. Ustedes pueden ayudar a su niño o niña a aprender más hablándole sobre las cosas que está haciendo en la escuela y sobre las nuevas letras y palabras que está aprendiendo. A continuación hay algunas actividades que le pueden servir para trabajar con su hijo o hija en casa.

Pensar y conversar

¿Qué leíste hoy? ¿Sobre qué se trataba el cuento?
¿Qué puedes hacer con manzanas?
¿Qué podrías hacer con las cosas que haces?

Actividades para la casa

El Vagón *Vv*

Dibujen un vagón en un pedazo de papel. Ayuden a su hijo o hija a encontrar letras *V* mayúsculas y *v* minúsculas en los titulares de periódicos y revistas. Encierren en un círculo la letras que encuentren y recórtenlas. Ayuden a su niño o niña a pegar las letras en el vagón.

Leyendo juntos

Los niños van a escuchar "The Apple Dumpling". Pidan a su hijo o hija que mencione las cosas con las que comercia la mujer para conseguir las manzanas. Lean otros cuentos sobre la compra y venta de cosas.

Lo que aprendí

Lean la nota que escribimos juntos.

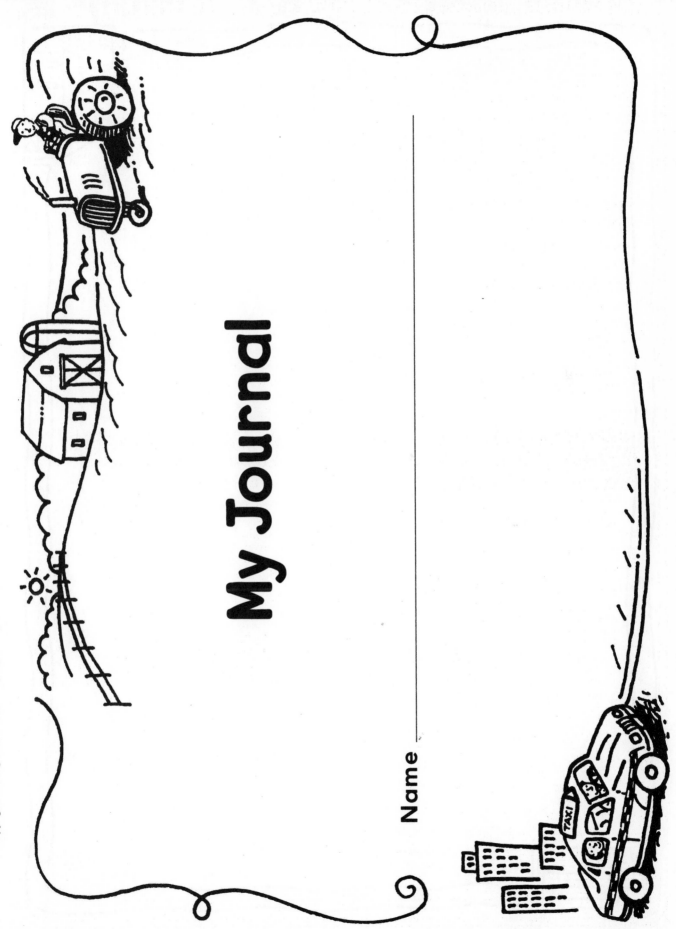

My Journal

Name

Border Paper

Shape Paper

In the City, In the Country

Center Sign-Up Sheet

Story Retelling Props for *My Farm*

Story Retelling Props for *My Farm*

Story Retelling Props for "The Billy Goat in the Garden"

Story Retelling Props for "The Billy Goat in the Garden"

Story Retelling Props for *Subway*

Story Retelling Props for *Subway*

Story Retelling Props for "City Mouse and Country Mouse"

Story Retelling Props for "City Mouse and Country Mouse"

Story Retelling Props for *Apple Farmer Annie*

Story Retelling Props for *Apple Farmer Annie*

Story Retelling Props for "The Apple Dumpling"

THEME 7: In the City, In the Country **237**

THEME 7: In the City, In the Country

Story Retelling Props for "The Apple Dumpling"

Theme 7: In the City, In the Country

Houghton Mifflin
PRE-K
Where Bright Futures Begin!

See the City,
See the Country

Annie Duffy

Think & Talk

What do you like about where you live?

ISBN 0-618513922
9 780618 513925
90000>

1-86116-LV PREK

HOUGHTON MIFFLIN

Title Code: 1-86116

COVER (t) Alan Schein/Corbis (b) Gavin Hellier/Getty Images. **Title page** Ryan McVay/PhotoDisc /Getty Images. **1** (t) Alan Schein/Corbis (b) Gavin Hellier/Getty Images. **2** Bruce Bukhardt/Corbis. **3** KazMori/The Image Bank/ Getty Images. **4** Ralf-Finn Hestoff/Corbis. **5** Comstock/Getty Images. **6** Will & Deni McIntyre/ Stone/Getty Images. **7** Brand X/ Getty Images. **8** Ryan McVay/PhotoDisc /Getty Images.

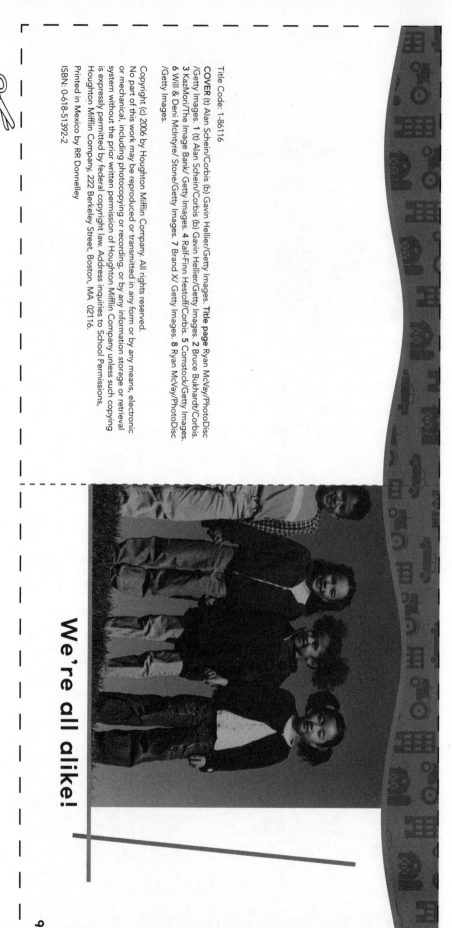

We're all alike!

9

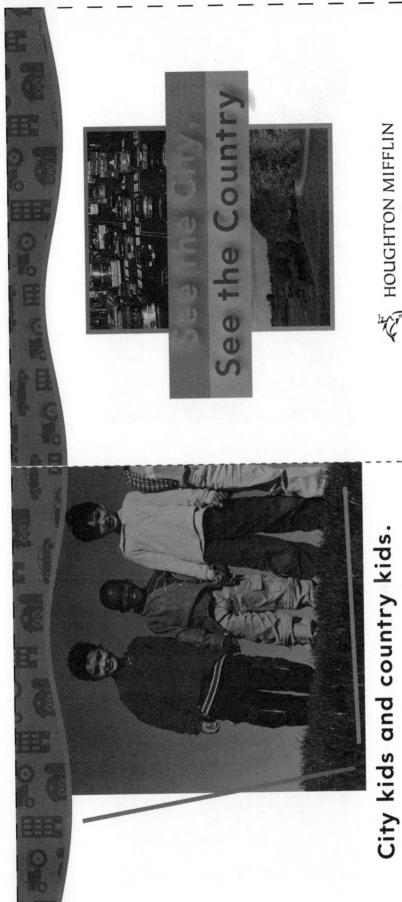

City kids and country kids.

8

HOUGHTON MIFFLIN

I see a city house.

I see a country street.

I see a country house.

I see a city street.

Little Hands Library *See the City, See the Country*

I see a city garden.

I see a country garden.

city

corn

country

cow

dollar

duck

eggs

farmer

Picture-Word Cards

office

penny

pig

quarter

quiet

rooster

transportation

sheep

Picture-Word Cards

sidewalk

stand

street

subway

tickets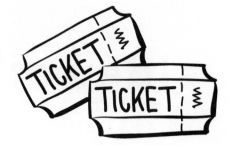

tractor

vehicles

vegetables

Let's Move!

CONTENTS

Let's Move!

lyrics by Jenny Reznick and Becky Manfredini
music by Harry Manfredini

Theme Song

Newsletter

Let's Move!

Dear Family,

This week _____ will learn about movement. Using the topic "Move with Me," we will read stories about the different ways we move, such as running, skipping, sliding, and jumping. You can help your child learn more by talking with her/him about the things he/she is doing at school and the new letters and words that he/she is learning. Here are some ways that you can work with your child at home.

What did you read today?
How did the characters in the story move?
What happened when the characters moved?
What is one way you like to move?

Home Activities

Jumping Jack or Jill

Make a stick puppet. Tell your child that the figure is *Jumping Jack* or *Jumping Jill* and that he/she likes the letters *Jj*. Look for *Jj*s in newspaper and magazine headlines with your child. Have her/him make the puppet "jump" each time he/she sees *Jj*.

"The Gingerbread Man"

Your child will listen to the story "The Gingerbread Man." Ask him/her to talk about the story and name the characters that try to catch the gingerbread man. Share other versions of this story with your child.

What I Learned

Here is a note from your child and her/his teacher.

Spanish Newsletter

Let's Move!

Querida familia:

Esta semana _____ va a aprender sobre el movimiento. Usando el tema "Move with Me" ("Muévete conmigo"), leeremos cuentos sobre las diferentes formas en que nos movemos: correr, brincar, resbalar y saltar. Ustedes pueden ayudar a su niño o niña a aprender más hablándole sobre las cosas que está haciendo en la escuela y sobre las nuevas letras y palabras que está aprendiendo. A continuación hay algunas actividades que le pueden servir para trabajar con su hijo o hija en casa.

Pensar y conversar

¿Qué leíste hoy?
¿Cómo se movían los personajes del cuento?
¿Qué pasaba cuando los personajes se movían?
¿De qué forma te gusta moverte?

Actividades para la casa

Juan o Juana

Hagan un muñeco de papel adherido a un pequeño palo. Digan a su hijo o hija que la figura es Juan juguetón o Juana juguetona y que a él o ella le gustan las letras *Jj*. Busquen *Jj* en titulares de periódicos o revistas. El muñeco brinca cada vez que ve *Jj*.

"The Gingerbread Man"

Su hijo o hija escuchará "The Gingerbread Man". Pídanle que hable del cuento y que mencione los personajes que intentan atrapar al hombrecito. Comenten con su niño o niña otras versiones de este cuento.

Lo que aprendí

Lean la nota que escribimos juntos.

Newsletter — WEEK 2

Let's Move!

Dear Family,

This week _____ will learn more about movement. Using the topic "Here We Go!," we will read stories about playing games that involve movement. You can help your child learn more by talking with her/him about the things he/she is doing at school and the new letters and words that he/she is learning. Here are some ways that you can work with your child at home.

 Think & Talk

What did you read about today?
What games did the characters play?
What was exciting about the story?
What game would you like us to play together?

Home Activities

Hh Hunt

Look at magazine and newspaper headlines with your child. Search for words that begin with capital *H* and small *h*. Circle the letters. Count the number of letters you find.

Moving and Playing

Children will listen to a book titled *We're Going on a Lion Hunt* this week. Ask your child to tell about the hunt the children from the book went on. Together, read other books about playing games that involve movement.

What I Learned

Here is a note from your child and her/his teacher.

Let's Move!

Querida familia:

Esta semana _____ va a aprender más sobre el movimiento. Usando el tema "Here We Go!" ("¡Aquí vamos!"), leeremos cuentos sobre juegos que involucran movimiento. Ustedes pueden ayudar a su niño o niña a aprender más hablándole sobre las cosas que está haciendo en la escuela y sobre las nuevas letras y palabras que está aprendiendo. A continuación hay algunas actividades que le pueden servir para trabajar con su hijo o hija en casa.

Pensar y conversar

¿Sobre qué leíste hoy?
¿Qué juegos jugaban los personajes?
¿Qué era lo más interesante del cuento?
¿Qué juego te gustaría que jugáramos juntos?

Actividades para la casa

Buscando *Hh*

Observen con su niño o niña los titulares de periódicos y revistas. Busquen palabras que comienzan con *H* mayúscula o *h* minúscula. Encierren las letras en un círculo. Cuenten el número de letras que encuentran.

Moverse y jugar

Los niños van a escuchar el libro *We're Going on a Lion Hunt* esta semana. Pidan a su hijo o hija que les cuente sobre la cacería a la que fueron las niñas del cuento. Lean juntos otros libros sobre juegos que involucran movimiento.

Lo que aprendí

Lean la nota que escribimos juntos.

Newsletter — WEEK 3

Let's Move!

Dear Family,

This week _____ will learn more about movement. Using the topic "Follow the Leader," we will read stories about following directions and solving problems. You can help your child learn more by talking with her/him about the things he/she is doing at school and the new letters and words that he/she is learning. Here are some ways that you can work with your child at home.

 Think & Talk

What did you read today?
What was the story about?
What was your favorite part of the story?
How did the characters in the story move?

Home Activities

Ii Poster

Look for *Ii* in newspaper and magazine headlines with your child. Cut out the letters and glue them to a large piece of paper. Encourage your child to circle capital *I* with a red crayon and small *i* with a green crayon.

Reading Together

Your child will listen to the book *Do Like a Duck Does!* this week. Ask her/him to tell what a duck does, such as quacks, waddles, and swims. Read other books about ducks, or play movement games, such as "Follow the Leader" with your child.

What I Learned

Here is a note from your child and her/his teacher.

Let's Move!

Querida familia:

Esta semana _____ va a aprender más sobre el movimiento. Usando el tema "Follow the Leader" ("Seguir al líder"), leeremos cuentos sobre seguir direcciones y resolver problemas. Ustedes pueden ayudar a su niño o niña a aprender más hablándole sobre las cosas que está haciendo en la escuela y sobre las nuevas letras y palabras que está aprendiendo. A continuación hay algunas actividades que le pueden servir para trabajar con su hijo o hija en casa.

Pensar y conversar

¿Qué leíste hoy?
¿Sobre qué se trataba el cuento?
¿Cuál fue tu parte favorita del cuento?
¿Cómo se movían los personajes del cuento?

Actividades para la casa

El afiche de la *Ii*

Busquen con su hijo o hija letras *Ii* en los titulares de periódicos y revistas. Recorten y peguen las letras a una hoja grande de papel. Animen a su hijo o hija a encerrar en un círculo de creyón rojo las *I* mayúsculas y de creyón verde las *i* minúsculas.

Leyendo juntos

Su hijo o hija escuchará esta semana *Do Like a Duck Does!* Pídanle que les cuente qué hace el pato, como su graznido, la forma como camina o como nada. Lean otros libros sobre patos o juegos que involucran movimiento, como "Seguir al líder".

Lo que aprendí

Lean la nota que escribimos juntos.

My Journal

Name

Border Paper

Shape Paper

Let's Move!

Center Sign-Up Sheet

_____

_____

_____

_____

_____

_____

Center Sign-Up Sheet

Story Retelling Props for *Thesaurus Rex*

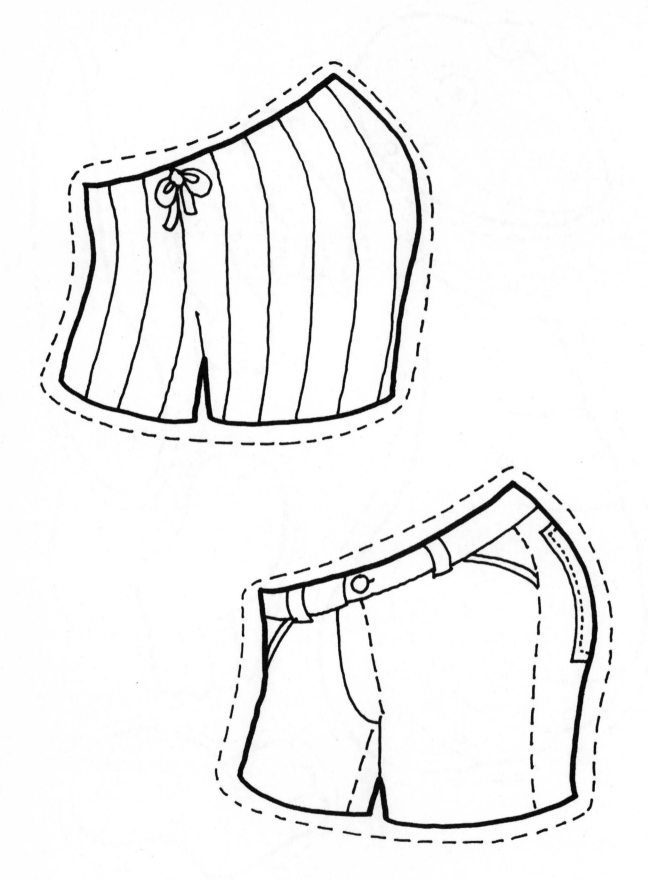

Story Retelling Props for *Thesaurus Rex*

Story Retelling Props for "The Gingerbread Man"

Story Retelling Props for "The Gingerbread Man"

Story Retelling Props for *We're Going on a Lion Hunt*

Story Retelling Props for *We're Going on a Lion Hunt*

Story Retelling Props for "Rabbit's Rope Tug"

Story Retelling Props for "Rabbit's Rope Tug"

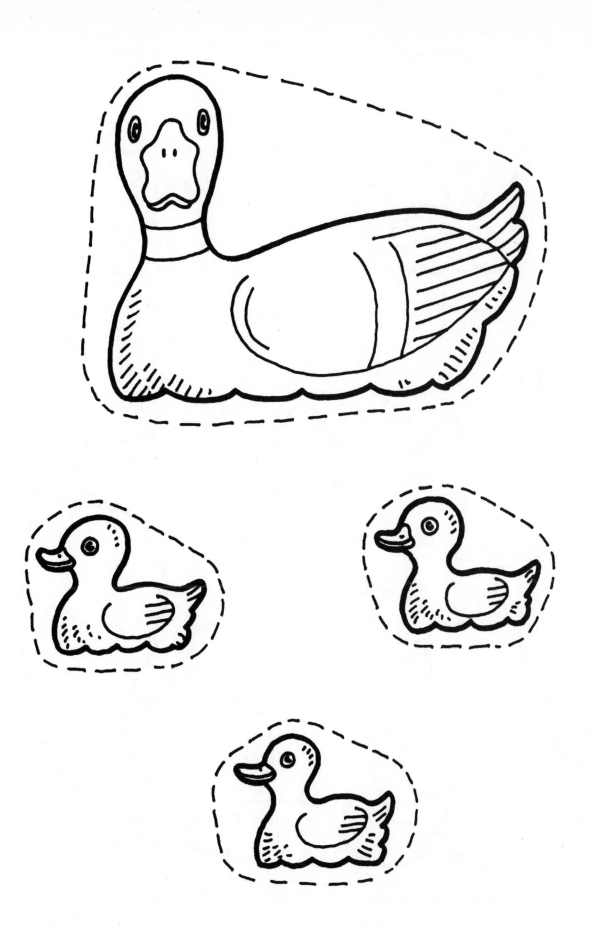

Story Retelling Props for *Do Like a Duck Does!*

Story Retelling Props for *Do Like a Duck Does!*

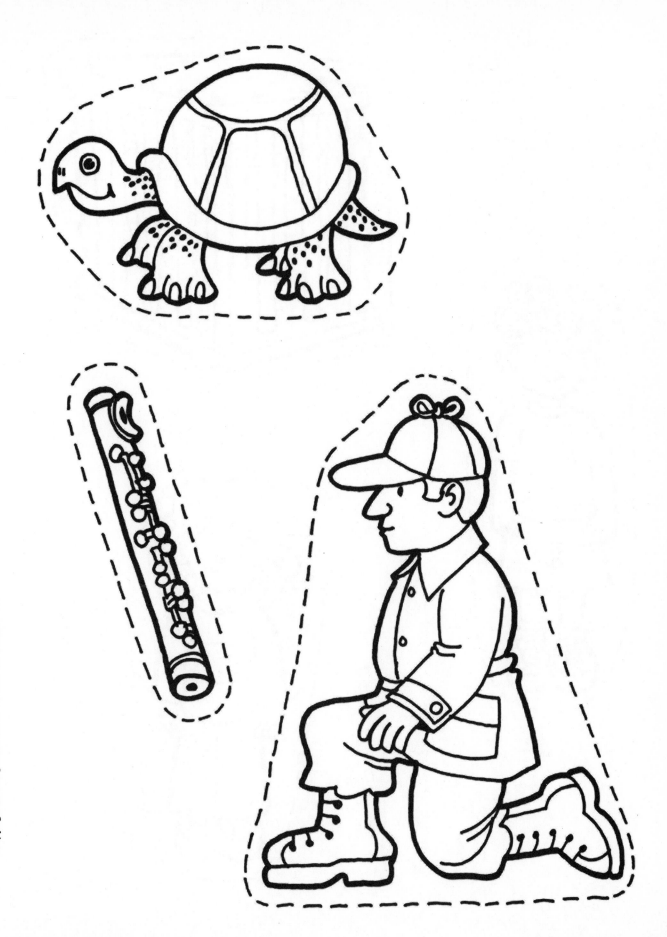

Story Retelling Props for "The Dancing Turtle"

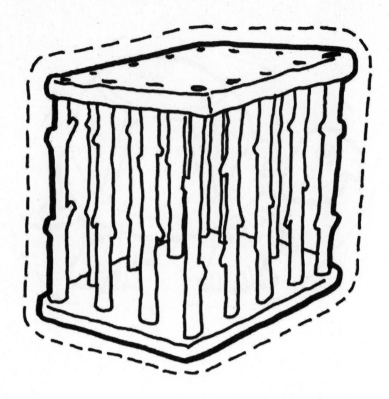

Story Retelling Props for "The Dancing Turtle"

Me in Motion

Coco Sargeant

Theme 8: Let's Move!

Houghton Mifflin PRE-K
Where Bright Futures Begin!

Think & Talk

What's your favorite way to move?

ISBN 0-618513930

9 780618 513932

1-86117-LV PREK

HOUGHTON MIFFLIN

Title Code: 1-86117

COVER/1 Corbis. **2** Frank Lane/Stone/Getty Images. **3** Wayne Eardley/Masterfile. **4** John W. Banagan/Getty Images. **5** David Madison/ Getty Images. **6** PhotoDisc/Getty Images. 7 Kevin Christopher Ou/Corbis. **8** Corbis. **9** Ariel Skelley/Corbis.

Copyright (c) 2006 by Houghton Mifflin Company. All rights reserved.

No part of this work may be reproduced or transmitted in any form or by any means, electronic or mechanical, including photocopying or recording, or by any information storage or retrieval system without the prior written permission of Houghton Mifflin Company unless such copying is expressly permitted by federal copyright law. Address inquiries to School Permissions, Houghton Mifflin Company, 222 Berkeley Street, Boston, MA 02116.

Printed in Mexico by RR Donnelley

ISBN: 0-618-51393-0

I can sleep, too. Goodnight!

9

Me in Motion

HOUGHTON MIFFLIN

Cats sleep.

8

2

Cheetahs run.

I can swim, too!

7

Little Hands Library *Me in Motion*

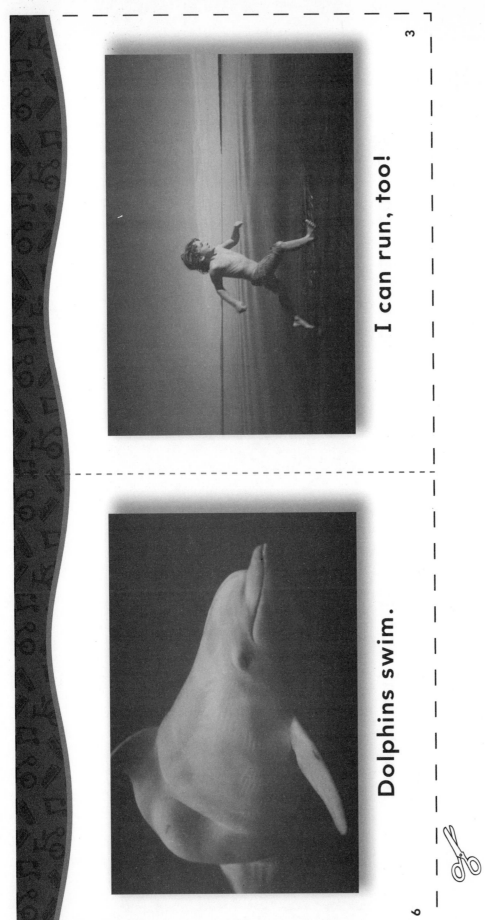

I can run, too!

3

Dolphins swim.

6

Kangaroos jump.

I can jump, too!

Little Hands Library *Me in Motion*

grass

lake

swamp

ball

balloon

jumps

hop

taxi

playground

slide

swing

costumes

dance

cymbal

drum

march

Picture-Word Cards

leader

beak

claws

ducklings

flute

jungle

tug of war

recipe

Teacher's Resource Book

Growing and Changing

CONTENTS

Growing Just Like Me!

lyrics by Jenny Reznick and Becky Manfredini
music by Harry Manfredini

Newsletter — WEEK 1

Growing and Changing

Dear Family,

This week _____ will learn about growing and changing. Using the topic "I'm Growing Every Day," we will read stories about growing up. You can help your child learn more by talking with her/him about the things he/she is doing at school and the new letters and words that he/she is learning. Here are some ways that you can work with your child at home.

Think & Talk

What did you read about today?
What did you learn about growing up today?
How have you grown since you were a baby?

Home Activities

Gg Poster

Gather *Gg*s from newspaper or magazine headlines with your child. At the end of the week, help him/her make a *Gg* poster. You can decorate the poster by adding pictures or photographs of things whose names start with *Gg*.

Change and Growth

Your child will listen to a book titled *Growing Like Me* this week. Ask her/him to tell about how frogs, ducks, and oak trees grow and change. Share other books about animals and things that grow and change with your child.

What I Learned

Here is a note from your child and her/his teacher.

Growing and Changing

Querida familia:

Esta semana _____ va a aprender sobre el crecimiento y el cambio. Usando el tema "I'm Growing Every Day" ("Crezco todos los días"), leeremos cuentos sobre el crecimiento. Ustedes pueden ayudar a su niño o niña a aprender más hablándole sobre las cosas que está haciendo en la escuela y sobre las nuevas letras y palabras que está aprendiendo. A continuación hay algunas actividades que le pueden servir para trabajar con su hijo o hija en casa.

Pensar y conversar

¿Sobre qué leíste hoy?
¿Qué aprendiste hoy sobre el crecimiento?
¿Cómo has crecido desde que eras un bebé?

Actividades para la casa

El afiche de la *Gg*

Recojan con su niño o niña letras *Gg* de los titulares de periódicos y revistas. Al final de la semana ayúdenlo a hacer un afiche de la *Gg*. Pueden decorar el afiche con imágenes o dibujos de objetos cuyos nombres comienzan con *Gg*.

Cambio y crecimiento

Su hijo o hija va a escuchar esta semana un libro titulado *Growing Like Me*. Pídanle que hable de cómo crecen y cambian las ranas, los patos y los robles. Compartan otros libros sobre animales y cosas que crecen y cambian.

Lo que aprendí

Lean la nota que escribimos juntos.

Newsletter — WEEK 2

Growing and Changing

Dear Family,

This week _____ will learn about changes in nature. Using the topic "Everything Changes," we will read stories about how things in nature grow and change. You can help your child learn more by talking with her/him about the things he/she is doing at school and the new letters and words that he/she is learning. Here are some ways that you can work with your child at home.

Think & Talk

What did you read today?
What was the story about?
What changes did you learn about?
What does a chrysalis look like?
Can you show me what a butterfly does?

Home Activities

Ee Egg

Draw an egg on drawing paper. Write *Ee* at the top of the paper and *Egg* at the bottom. Point out that *Egg* begins with *E*. Look for *Ee*s in newspaper and magazine headlines with your child. Cut them out and help your child glue them on the egg.

Butterflies in Books

Your child will listen to the story *Waiting for Wings* this week. Ask her/him to tell you about the stages of growth a butterfly goes through. Share other books about butterflies with your child.

What I Learned

Here is a note from your child and her/his teacher.

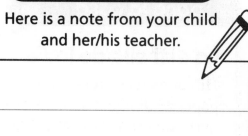

Spanish Newsletter

WEEK 2 — **Growing and Changing**

Querida familia:

Esta semana _____ va a aprender sobre los cambios en la naturaleza. Usando el tema "Everything Changes" ("Todo cambia"), leeremos cuentos sobre cómo crecen y cambian las cosas de la naturaleza. Ustedes pueden ayudar a su niño o niña a aprender más hablándole sobre las cosas que está haciendo en la escuela y sobre las nuevas letras y palabras que está aprendiendo. A continuación hay algunas actividades que le pueden servir para trabajar con su hijo o hija en casa.

Pensar y conversar

¿Qué leíste hoy?

¿Sobre qué se trataba el cuento?

¿Sobre qué cambios aprendiste hoy? ¿Cómo es una crisálida?

¿Puedes mostrarme qué hace una mariposa?

Actividades para la casa

La estrella de la *Ee*

Dibujen una estrella de mar en papel de dibujo. Escriban *Ee* en la parte superior y *Estrella de Mar* en la inferior. Muéstrenle a su hijo o hija que *Estrella* comienza con *E*. Busquen *Ee* en los titulares de periódicos y revistas con su niño o niña. Córtenlas y ayuden a su niño o niña a pegarlas sobre la estrella.

Mariposas en los libros

Su hijo o hija escuchará el libro *Waiting for Wings.* Pídanle que les cuente sobre las etapas de crecimiento de las mariposas. Compartan otros libros sobre mariposas.

Lo que aprendí

Lean la nota que escribimos juntos.

Newsletter

WEEK 3

Growing and Changing

Dear Family,

This week _____ will learn about spring. Using the topic "Look, It's Spring!," we will read stories about how plants and animals grow and change in the spring. You can help your child learn more by talking with her/him about the things he/she is doing at school and the new letters and words that he/she is learning. Here are some ways that you can work with your child at home.

Think & Talk

What did you read today?
What did you like best about the story?
What grows and changes in the spring?
What would you like us to plant in the spring?

Home Activities

Looking for *Dd*

Look for *Dd*s on food packaging, such as cereal boxes and labels on cans. You can also look for *Dd*s on signs around your neighborhood. Encourage your child to tell you whether the letter they found is a capital *D* or a small *d*.

Reading Together

Your child will listen to the classic folktale "Jack and the Beanstalk" this week. Read other versions of this story with your child. Talk about how the stories are alike and different.

What I Learned

Here is a note from your child and her/his teacher.

Spanish Newsletter

Growing and Changing

Querida familia:

Esta semana _____ va a aprender sobre la primavera. Usando el tema "Look, It's Spring!" ("¡Mira, es primavera!"), leeremos cuentos sobre cómo crecen y cambian las plantas y los animales en primavera. Ustedes pueden ayudar a su niño o niña a aprender más hablándole sobre las cosas que está haciendo en la escuela y sobre las nuevas letras y palabras que está aprendiendo. A continuación hay algunas actividades que le pueden servir para trabajar con su hijo o hija en casa.

Pensar y conversar

¿Qué leíste hoy?

¿Qué fue lo que más te gustó del cuento?

¿Qué crece y cambia en la primavera?

¿Qué te gustaría que sembráramos en la primavera?

Actividades para la casa

Buscando *Dd*

Busquen letras *Dd* en empaques de alimentos o en las etiquetas de comida enlatada. También pueden buscar *Dd* en las señales de tránsito en su vecindario. Animen a su niño o niña que les diga si la letra que están viendo es una *D* mayúscula o una *d* minúscula.

Leyendo juntos

Su hijo o hija escuchará esta semana la leyenda clásica "Jack and the Beanstalk". Lean otras versiones de este cuento con su niño o niña. Hablen sobre las diferencias y similitudes entre ellas.

Lo que aprendí

Lean la nota que escribimos juntos.

My Journal

Name _____

Journal Cover

Border Paper

Shape Paper

Growing and Changing

Center Sign-Up Sheet

_____

_____

_____

_____

_____

_____

Center Sign-Up Sheet

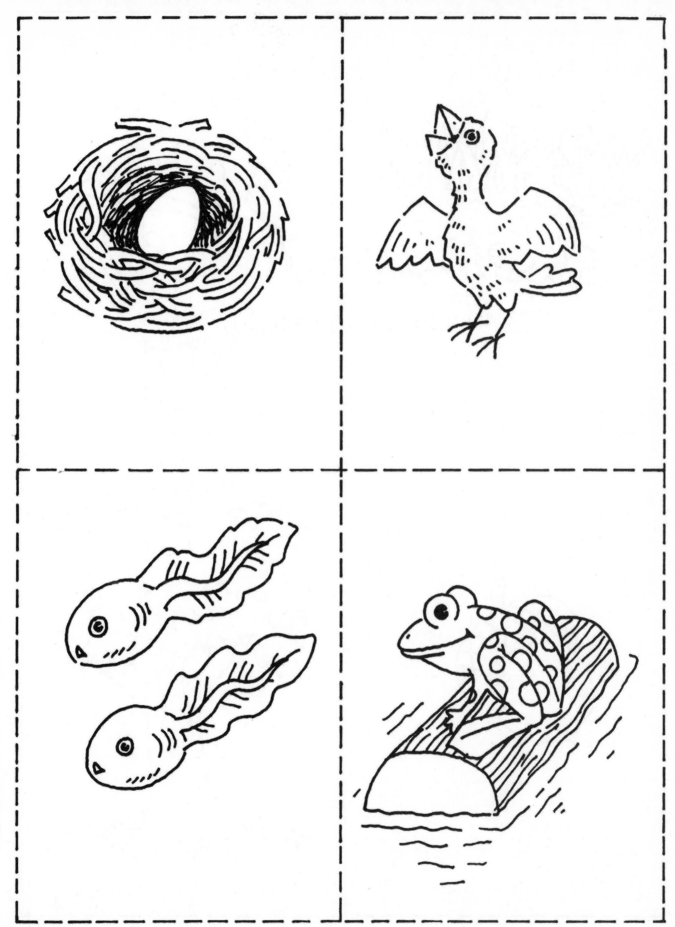

Story Retelling Props for *Growing Like Me*

Story Retelling Props for *Growing Like Me*

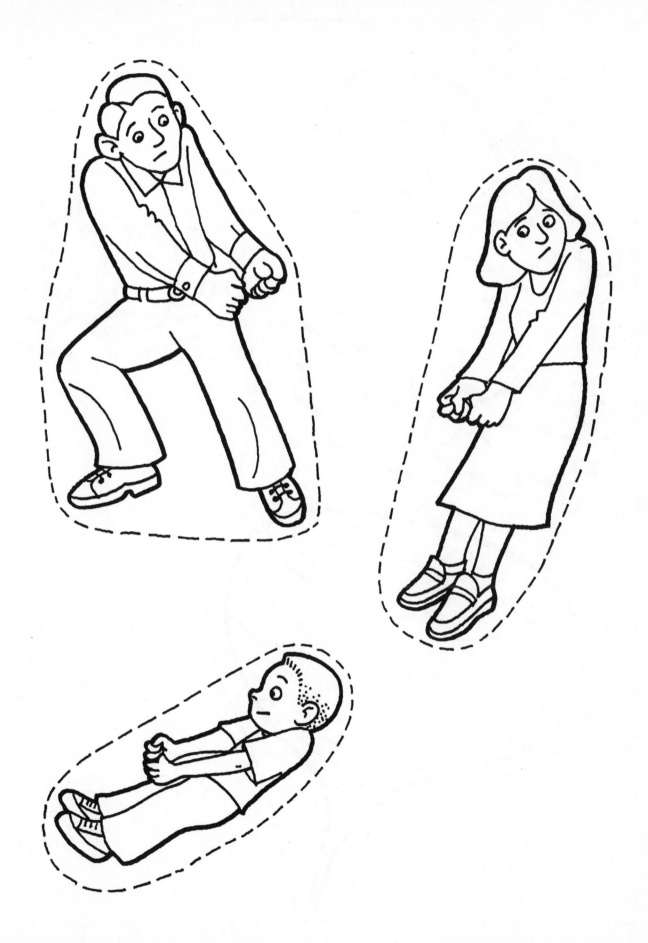

Story Retelling Props for "The Gigantic Turnip"

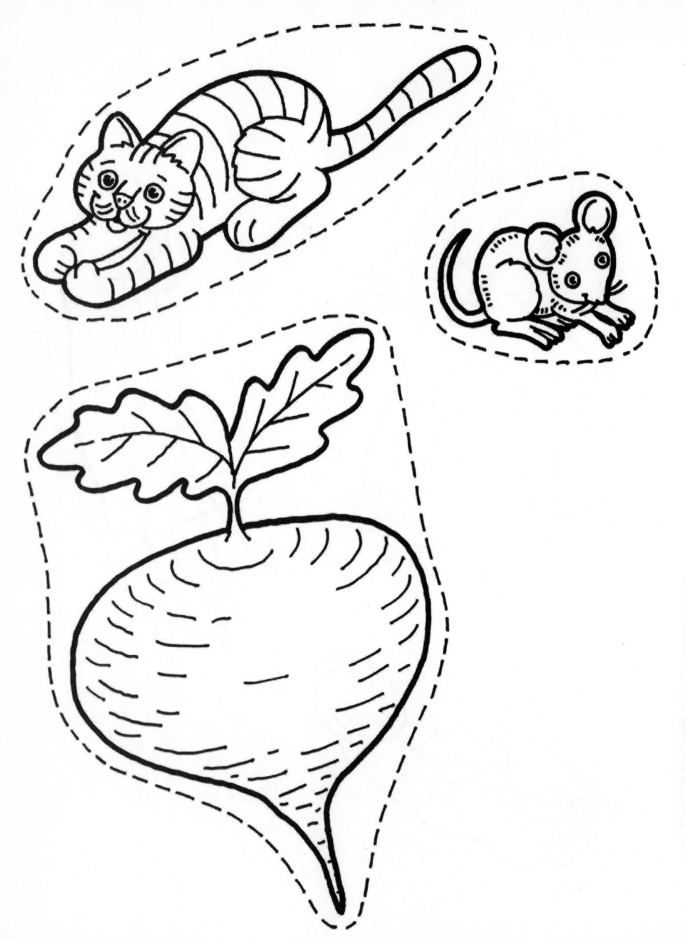

Story Retelling Props for "The Gigantic Turnip"

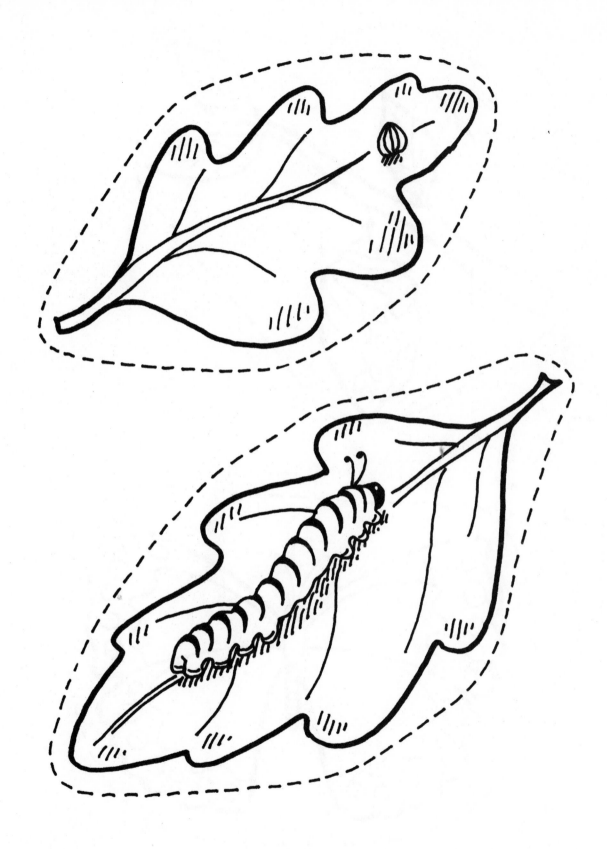

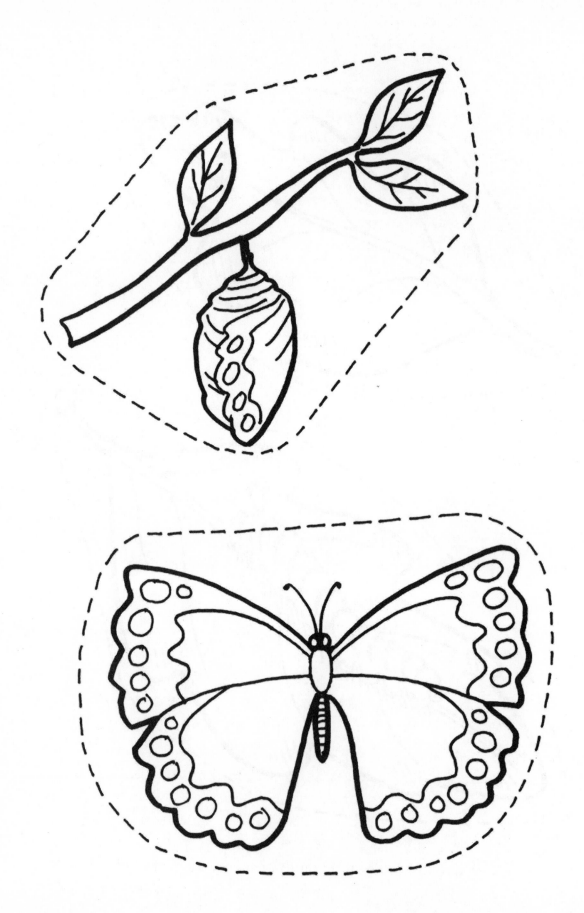

Story Retelling Props for *Waiting for Wings*

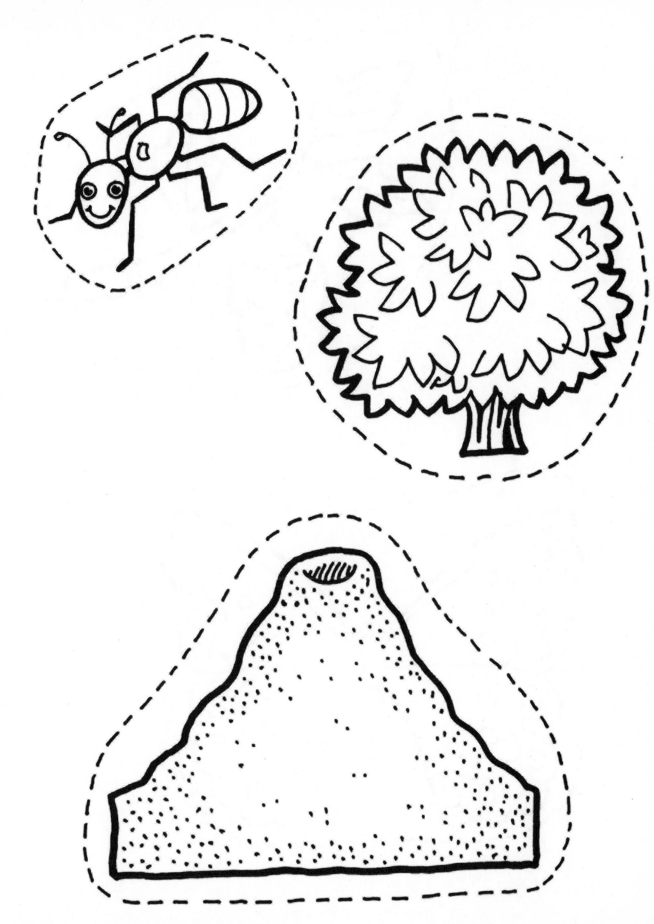

Story Retelling Props for "The Ant and the Chrysalis"

THEME 9: Growing and Changing 305

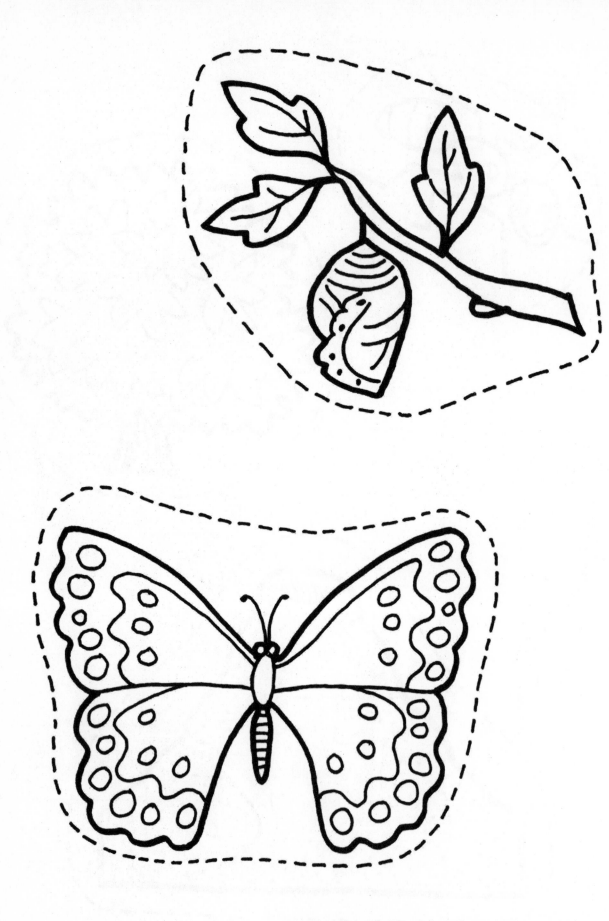

Story Retelling Props for "The Ant and the Chrysalis"

Story Retelling Props for *Spring Song*

Story Retelling Props for *Spring Song*

Story Retelling Props for "Jack and the Beanstalk"

Story Retelling Props for "Jack and the Beanstalk"

GrowingUp

Jennifer Daniels

Houghton Mifflin
PRE-K
Where Bright Futures Begin!

Theme 9: Growing and Changing

Think & Talk

What can you do that babies can't do?

ISBN 0-618513949

9 780618 513949

1-86118-LV PREK

HOUGHTON MIFFLIN

Title Code: 1-86118

COVER Ken Huang/The Image Bank/ Getty Images. 1 Jim Arbogast/ PhotoDisc/Getty Images.
2 Andersen/Ross/Brand X/Getty Images. 3 Tim Platt/ The Image Bank/ Getty Images. 4 Ryan
McVay/PhotoDisc/Getty Images. 5 Roger Charity/Stone/Getty Images. 6 Corbis. 7 Picturequest.
8 Camille Tokerud/Stone/Getty Images. 9 Picturequest.

Copyright (c) 2006 by Houghton Mifflin Company. All rights reserved.
No part of this work may be reproduced or transmitted in any form or by any means, electronic
or mechanical, including photocopying or recording, or by any information storage or retrieval
system without the prior written permission of Houghton Mifflin Company unless such copying
is expressly permitted by federal copyright law. Address inquiries to School Permissions,
Houghton Mifflin Company, 222 Berkeley Street, Boston, MA 02116.

Printed in Mexico by RR Donnelley

ISBN: 0-618-51394-9

What can you do?

9

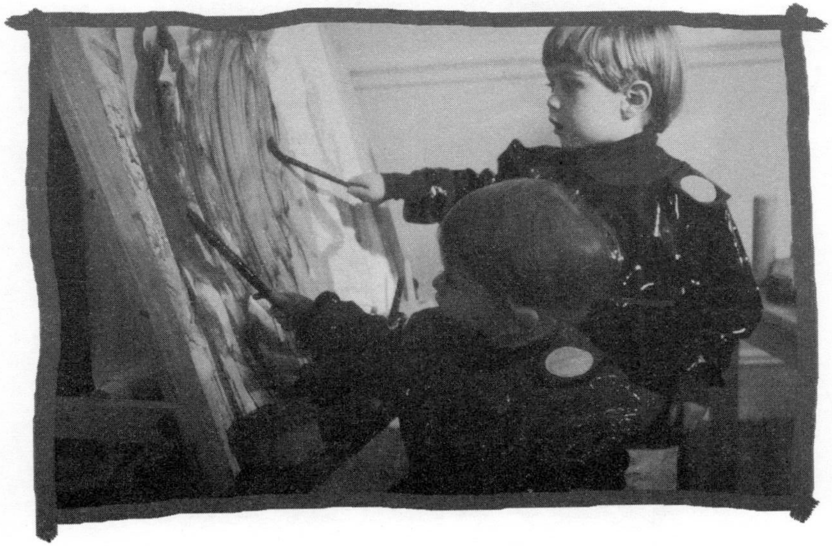

You're growing up, too!

8

Growing Up

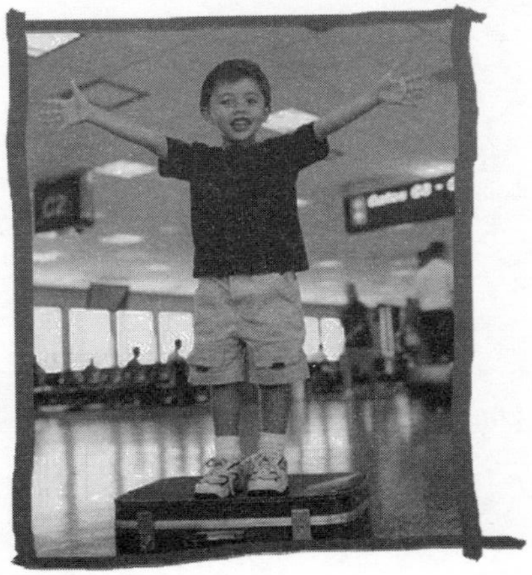

HOUGHTON MIFFLIN

2

I can brush my teeth.

I can write my name.

7

I can get dressed.

3

I can play safely.

6

Little Hands Library *Growing Up*

4

I can tie my shoes.

I can help my brother.

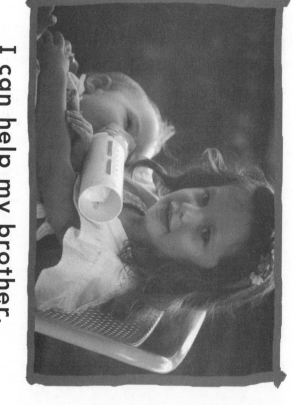

5

Little Hands Library *Growing Up*

baby

caterpillar

garden

turnip

Picture-Word Cards

fruits

milk

den

toothbrush

hatch

Earth

chrysalis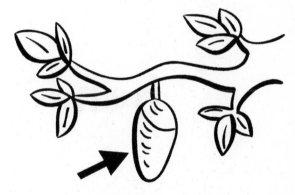

flower bud

egg

seed

hen

shell

Picture-Word Cards

spring

nest

sun

flower

jacket

fox

summer

winter

Picture-Word Cards

Teacher's Resource Book

Ready for Kindergarten!

CONTENTS

Kindergarten!

lyrics by Jenny Reznick and Becky Manfredini
music by Harry Manfredini

Newsletter

Ready for Kindergarten!

Dear Family,

This week _____ will celebrate what we have learned about letters and words. Using the topic "Now I Know My ABCs," we will read alphabet books. You can help your child learn more by talking with him/her about the things he/she is doing at school and the new letters and words that he/she is learning. Here are some ways that you can work with your child at home.

Think & Talk

Can you see some words in our home?
Do you know the names of some of the letters in those words?
What other letters do you know?

Home Activities

Ll Hunt

Look around your home for objects whose names begin with small *l*, such as *lamp* and *lock*. Write the names of the objects on index cards. Help your child write small *l* in each word. Post the labels near each object.

Patterns

Look for patterns around your house and name them with your child. For example, say *The wallpaper pattern is green, white, green, white.* Look for more patterns in photographs and illustrations in books you read together.

What I Learned

Here is a note from your child and her/his teacher.

Spanish Newsletter

— WEEK 1 —

Ready for Kindergarten!

Querida familia:

Esta semana _____ va a celebrar lo que hemos aprendido sobre las letras y palabras. Usando el tema "Now I Know My ABCs" ("Ahora sé el alfabeto"), leeremos libros de alfabeto. Ustedes pueden ayudar a su niño o niña a aprender más hablándole sobre las cosas que está haciendo en la escuela y sobre las nuevas letras y palabras que está aprendiendo. A continuación hay algunas actividades que le pueden servir para trabajar con su hijo o hija en casa.

Pensar y conversar

¿Puedes ver algunas palabras en nuestra casa?
¿Conoces el nombre de algunas de las letras en esas palabras?
¿Qué otras letras conoces?

Actividades para la casa

Buscando *Ll*

Busquen en su hogar objetos cuyos nombres empiezan con *l* minúscula, como por ejemplo *lámpara* y *libro*. Escriban el nombre de los objetos en tarjetas. Ayuden a su niño o niña a escribir la letra *l* minúscula en cada palabra. Coloquen cada tarjeta sobre cada objeto.

Patrones

Busquen patrones en la casa y descríbanlos con su hijo o hija. Digan, por ejemplo, *El patrón del papel tapiz es verde, blanco, verde, blanco.* Busquen más patrones en fotografías e ilustraciones en libros.

Lo que aprendí

Lean la nota que escribimos juntos.

Newsletter

WEEK 2

Ready for Kindergarten!

Dear Family,

This week _____ will learn more about numbers and shapes. Using the topic "We Count!" we will read counting books and talk about how numbers are used. You can help your child learn more by talking with him/her about the things he/she is doing at school and the new letters and words that he/she is learning. Here are some ways that you can work with your child at home.

Think & Talk

What numbers do you see in our home?
Where are they?
Let's count. What things would you like to count?

Home Activities

Nn Hunt

Write the word *Numbers* at the top of a piece of construction paper. Write number words from one to ten on the paper. Read the words with your child. Have your child find and circle the *Nn*s in the words. Count the *Nn*s you find.

Finding Numbers

Look for numbers around your neighborhood and when you go on errands. Have your child name the numbers. Talk about what the numbers mean.

What I Learned

Here is a note from your child and her/his teacher.

Spanish Newsletter — WEEK 2

Querida familia:

Esta semana _____ va aprender más sobre los números y las formas. Usando el tema "We Count!" ("¡Contamos!"), leeremos libros de contar y hablaremos sobre las formas como se usan los números. Ustedes pueden ayudar a su niño o niña a aprender más hablándole sobre las cosas que está haciendo en la escuela y sobre las nuevas letras y palabras que está aprendiendo. A continuación hay algunas actividades que le pueden servir para trabajar con su hijo o hija en casa.

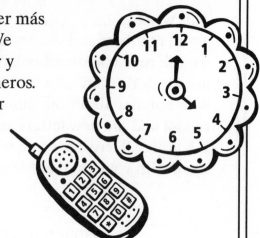

Pensar y conversar

¿Qué números ves en nuestra casa?
¿Dónde están? Contemos.
¿Qué cosas te gustaría contar?

Actividades para la casa

Buscando *Nn*

Escriban la palabra *Números* en la parte superior de una hoja de cartulina. En la misma hoja, escriban en palabras los números del uno al diez. Lean las palabras con su niño o niña. Hagan que él o ella encuentre y encierre en un círculo las letras *Nn* en las palabras. Cuenten las letras *Nn* que encuentren.

Encontrando números

Busquen números en su vecindario o cuando salgan a hacer un mandado. Hagan que su hijo o hija nombre los números. Conversen sobre lo que significa cada número.

Lo que aprendí

Lean la nota que escribimos juntos.

Newsletter — WEEK 3

Dear Family,

This week _____ will revisit what he/she has learned this year. Using the topic "Off to Kindergarten!" we will read stories about things he/she can do now and what he/she will do in Kindergarten. You can help your child learn more by talking with him/her about the things he/she is doing at school and the new letters and words that he/she is learning. Here are some ways that you can work with your child at home.

Think & Talk

What letters do you know? Let's say the alphabet together. What numbers do you know? Let's count to ten together. What is your favorite thing to do at school?

Home Activities

Kk Collage

Write *Kk* at the top of a large piece of paper. Help your child find pictures of objects whose names begin with *Kk* in newspapers, catalogs, and magazines. Make a collage with the pictures. You can also draw your own pictures.

Shape Books

Have your child draw shapes on pieces of drawing or construction paper. Staple the pages together to make a shape book. Your child can color or decorate each shape. Encourage her/him to name each one.

What I Learned

Here is a note from your child and her/his teacher.

Spanish Newsletter

Ready for Kindergarten!

Querida familia:

Esta semana _____ va a repasar lo que aprendió este año. Usando el tema "Off to Kindergarten!" ("¡Vamos a Kindergarten!"), leeremos cuentos sobre las cosas que él o ella puede hacer ahora y sobre lo que va a hacer en Kindergarten. Ustedes pueden ayudar a su niño o niña a aprender más hablándole sobre las cosas que está haciendo en la escuela y sobre las nuevas letras y palabras que está aprendiendo. A continuación hay algunas actividades que le pueden servir para trabajar con su hijo o hija en casa.

Pensar y conversar

¿Qué letras conocces? Digamos juntos el alfabeto.
¿Qué números conoces? Contemos juntos hasta diez.
¿Qué es lo que más te gusta hacer en la escuela?

Actividades para la casa

Afiche de la *Kk*

Escriban *Kk* en la parte superior de una hoja grande de papel. Ayuden a su hijo o hija a encontrar imágenes de cosas cuyos nombres empiezan con *Kk* en catálogos, revistas o periódicos. Hagan un afiche con las imágenes que encuentren. También pueden hacer sus propios dibujos.

Libros de formas

Hagan que su hijo o hija dibuje formas en hojas de cartulina o de papel de dibujo. Engrapen las hojas para hacer un libro de formas. Su niño o niña puede colorear o decorar cada forma. Anímelo/a a nombrar cada una de las formas.

Lo que aprendí

Lean la nota que escribimos juntos.

My Journal

Name _____

Border Paper

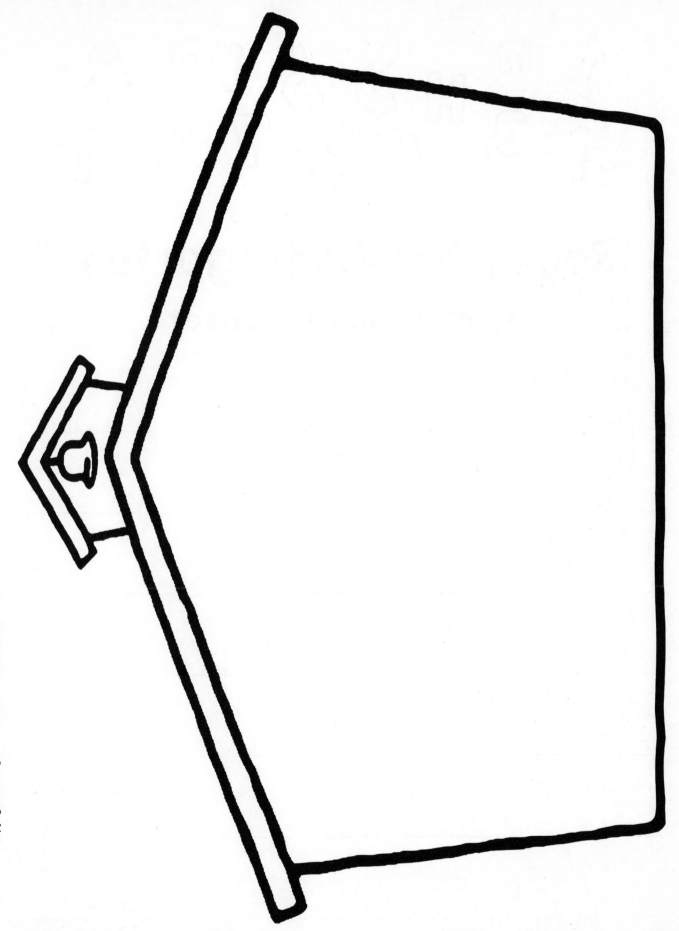

Shape Paper

Ready for Kindergarten!

Center Sign-Up Sheet

_____

_____

_____

_____

_____

_____

Story Retelling Props for *Chicka Chicka Boom Boom*

336   THEME 10: Ready for Kindergarten!   Story Retelling Props for *Chicka Chicka Boom Boom*

Story Retelling Props for "The Tortoise and the Hare"

Story Retelling Props for "The Tortoise and the Hare"

Story Retelling Props for _Little Rabbits' First Number Book_

Story Retelling Props for *Little Rabbits' First Number Book*

Story Retelling Props for "Counting Leopard's Spots"

Story Retelling Props for "Counting Leopard's Spots"

Story Retelling Props for *We Can!*

Story Retelling Props for "The Ugly Duckling"

Story Retelling Props for "The Ugly Duckling"

Theme 10: Ready for Kindergarten!

Title Code: 1-86119
COVER Artville; PhotoDisc. **6-8** PhotoDisc. **9** Artville; PhotoDisc.

Copyright (c) 2006 by Houghton Mifflin Company. All rights reserved.
No part of this work may be reproduced or transmitted in any form or by any means, electronic or mechanical, including photocopying or recording, or by any information storage or retrieval system without the prior written permission of Houghton Mifflin Company unless such copying is expressly permitted by federal copyright law. Address inquiries to School Permissions, Houghton Mifflin Company, 222 Berkeley Street, Boston, MA 02116.

Printed in Mexico by RR Donnelley
ISBN: 0-618-51395-7

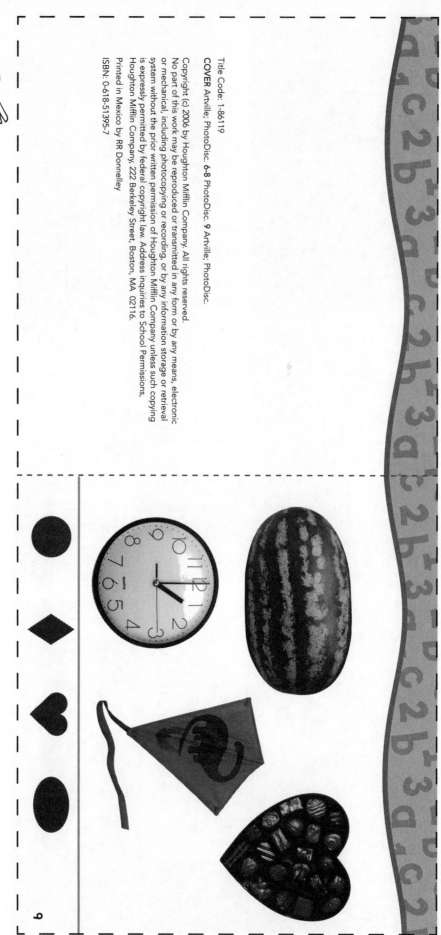

9

What shapes can you find?

Look What I Know!

HOUGHTON MIFFLIN

8

What letters can you name?

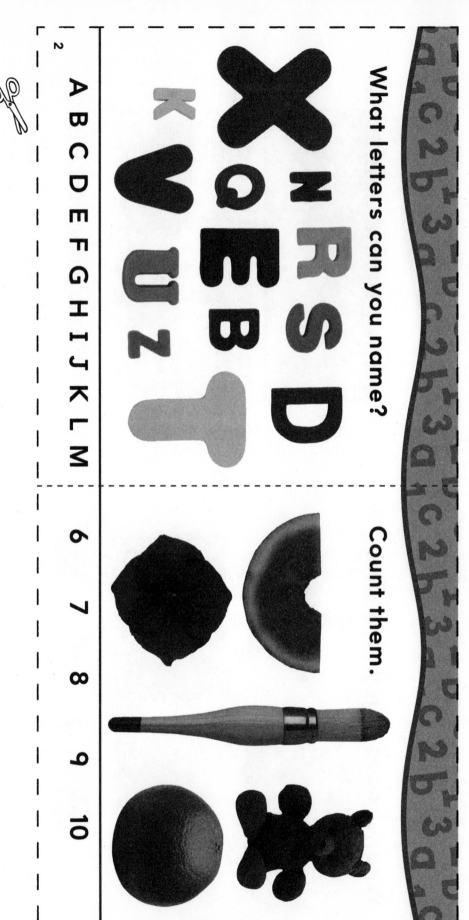

Count them.

N R S D
X Q E B
K V U Z T

A B C D E F G H I J K L M   6 7 8 9 10

2   7

How many things do you see?

T J P L A W
I Y G M C
O F G M H

N O P Q R S T U V W X Y Z

3

1 2 3 4 5

6

What numbers do you know?

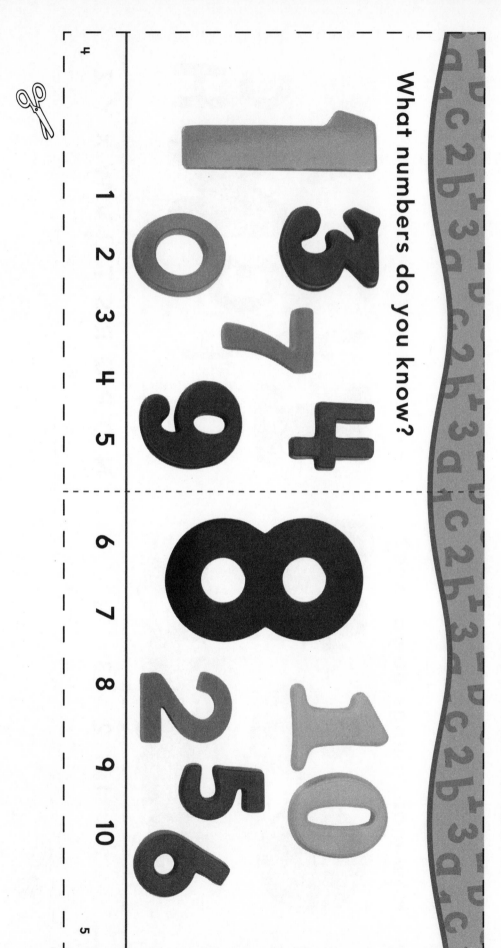

1 2 3 4 5 6 7 8 9 10

letters

ruler

book

bicycle

flowers

school bus

moon

stars

Picture-Word Cards

school

shapes

spots

computer

microwave

telephone

television

clock

Picture-Word Cards

music

magnifying glass

mouse

hatch

flock

swans

scale

blackboard

Picture-Word Cards

Math
Concept Cards

CONTENTS

MATH CONCEPT CARD

1

Circles and Ovals

Find the circles. Find the ovals. Tell about them.

Circles and Ovals

Circles and Ovals

LEARNING GOALS

Geometry
- recognizes and names shapes
- uses terms related to shapes
- compares and models shapes

Math Vocabulary
circle
oval
shape

▶ Cover the pictures of the platter and the placemat. Have children name the other objects.

▶ Trace the circle outline on each object with your finger. Explain that this *shape* is called a *circle*. Tell children that a *circle* is a round shape that has a curved line.

▶ Call on children to name and trace the circle outline on each object.

▶ Trace the *oval* shape on the platter and placemat. Help children understand that an oval is a curved line too, but it is not a circle because it is not perfectly round. Ask children to name and trace the oval outline on each object.

▶ Have children tell how the shapes are the same and how they are different.

▶ Place the card in the Math Center. Children can use the photograph to find and draw other circles and ovals in the classroom.

Make It Easier Cut out several circles and ovals. Have children trace the edge of the shapes with a finger to reinforce their ability to identify them.

Make It Harder Challenge children to find other circles and ovals in the classroom. Invite them to share where they found the shapes.

Lesson Tips

■ Using two pencils tied together with string, show children that each point on the circle's outline is the same distance from the center. Tell them that this is what makes the shape a *circle*. Using the simple compass, help children understand that an oval is not a circle because it is not perfectly round.

■ Provide children with many opportunities to identify circles and ovals in books, posters, and other classroom objects.

■ Play a game in which partners trace a circle or an oval on each other's backs. Children can guess which shape their partners have traced.

Home Connection

Post Math Card 1 on your family communication board so that families know what children are learning about shapes. Encourage them to help children find these shapes at home or when driving in the car.

What shapes do you see? Tell about them.

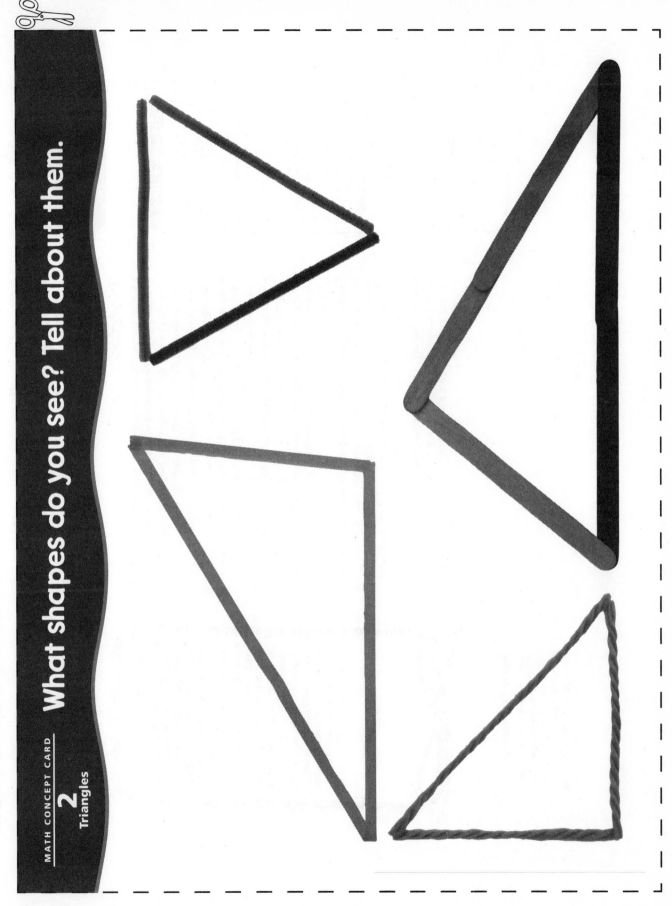

Triangles

LEARNING GOALS

Geometry
- recognizes and names shapes
- uses terms related to shapes
- compares and models shapes

Math Vocabulary
corner
side
triangle

Triangles

▶ Discuss the photograph with children. Explain that it shows many different shapes called *triangles*. Explain that a triangle is a shape with 3 *sides* and 3 *corners*. Help children understand the meaning of the terms sides and corners.

▶ Trace a triangle and lead children in counting the number of sides and corners.

▶ Repeat for the other examples. Point out that each shape has three sides and three corners, and that this is what makes each a *triangle*.

▶ Point out pairs of triangles and ask children to tell how they are the same and how they are different.

▶ Place the card in the Math Center. Children can use the photograph as a reference to find and draw other triangles in the classroom.

Make It Easier Display six to eight circle and triangle attribute blocks. Ask children to identify and then sort the blocks. Then have children use a finger to trace the circles and the sides of several triangles. Ask them to count the number of sides and corners of each triangle.

Make It Harder Challenge children to find triangles in the classroom. Invite them to share where they found the shapes. Ask children to compare a triangle they found with a triangle on the Math Card.

Lesson Tips

■ When introducing the terms *sides* and *corners*, trace one side of a triangle with your finger and explain that a line segment like this is called a *side*. Then point to a corner and explain that a *corner* is where two sides come together.

■ Play a game in which pairs tape a cutout shape on each other's back. They trace the outline of the shape and partners can guess the name of the shape.

■ Provide children with many opportunities to identify triangles in books, posters, and other classroom objects. Frequent exposure will help them to identify the shapes easily.

Home Connection

 Post Math Card 2 on your family communication board so that families know what children are learning about shapes. Encourage them to help children find these shapes at home or on a shopping trip.

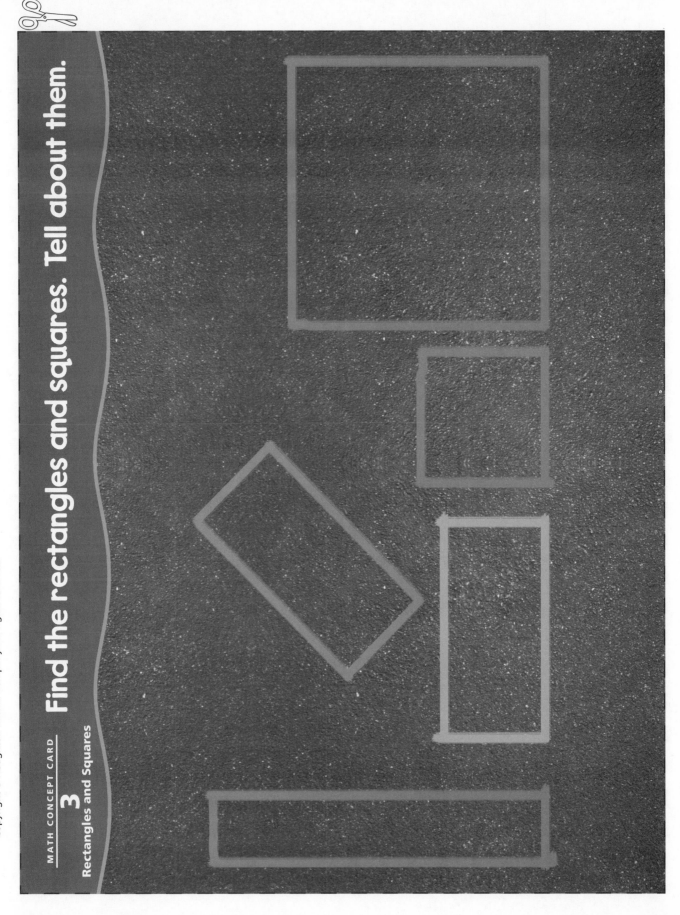

MATH CONCEPT CARD

3

Rectangles and Squares

Find the rectangles and squares. Tell about them.

Find the rectangles and squares. Tell about them.

Rectangles and Squares

▶ Discuss the photograph with children. Explain that it shows a number of shapes called *rectangles*. Explain that a rectangle is a shape with four sides and four square corners. Help children understand the meaning of the terms *sides* and *corners*. Explain that a square corner looks like an *L*.

▶ Trace the first rectangle and lead children in counting the number of sides and corners.

▶ Repeat for the first square shape. Point out this shape a special kind of rectangle called a *square*. Explain that it has four sides and four square corners, but all of the sides are the same length. Explain that four corners and four sides all the same length make this a *square*.

▶ Point out pairs of rectangles and squares and ask children to say how they are the same and how they are different.

▶ Place the card in the Math Center. Children can use the photograph as a reference for finding and drawing rectangles and squares in the classroom.

Make It Easier Display six to eight rectangle and square attribute blocks. Have children compare them to help reinforce their ability to identify them. Ask them to sort the shapes into two groups: squares and rectangles that are not squares.

Make It Harder Challenge children to find rectangles and squares in the classroom. Invite them to share where they found the shapes.

LEARNING GOALS

Geometry/Spatial Sense
- recognizes and names shapes
- uses terms related to shapes
- compares and models shapes

Math Vocabulary
corner
rectangle
side
square

Lesson Tips

- Trace one side of a rectangle with your finger, telling children that this part (the line segment) is called a *side*. Then point to a corner and explain that a corner is where two sides come together.

- Place attribute blocks or cutouts of a variety of shapes in a bag. Invite children to choose a shape, keeping it hidden. Children can use their fingers to explore the shape and count its sides and corners, if any, to identify it. They can show the shape so the group can verify the shape's identity.

- During snack time, serve triangular and square crackers. Children can compare the number of corners and sides.

- Place shape cookie cutters at the sand table, so that children can experiment modeling different shapes.

Home Connection

 Post Math Card 3 on your family communication board so that families know what children are learning about shapes. Encourage them to help children find rectangular shapes at home and in their neighborhood.

What do you see? Tell where it is.

What do you see? Tell where it is.

LEARNING GOALS

Geometry/Spatial Sense
- understands and describes positions

Math Vocabulary

above
below
beside
bottom
middle
next to
on
top

Position Words

▶ Point to and name each toy on the bookcase. Explain that toys are on different shelves of the bookcase.

▶ Point to the (teddy bear). Say: I see a (teddy bear). It is on the (top) shelf of the bookcase. It is *next to* the (dog).

▶ Repeat for other toys on the bookcase. Use the Math Vocabulary to describe the positions. Ask questions, such as: **What is on the *top* shelf? What is *beside* the dog?** Have children point to each object you describe.

▶ Place the card in the Math Center. Children can ask each other questions about the objects on the shelves.

Make It Easier Take two common objects and put them in relative positions that can be described using the vocabulary words. Ask children where each object is. Move objects into new positions and repeat.

Make It Harder Challenge pairs of children to arrange a variety of objects and ask their partner to describe the positions. Both partners should take a turn arranging and then describing the positions of the objects.

Lesson Tips

- Arrange a small set of objects on the shelves of a bookcase. Invite children to describe the positions of the objects. Repeat with the same objects in different arrangements.

- Provide children with many opportunities to describe the relative positions of classroom objects. Frequent practice will help them to understand and use the vocabulary for position words with greater ease.

Home Connection

Post Math Card 4 on your family communication board so that families know what children are learning about position words. Encourage them to help children use these words to describe objects on shelves at home as they help in the kitchen or clean up their toys.

MATH CONCEPT CARD
5
Position Words

Who do you see? Tell where each child is standing.

LEARNING GOALS

Geometry/Spatial Sense

- understands and describes positions
- identifies first, middle, and last

Math Vocabulary

behind
between
first
in back
in front
last
middle
next to

Position Words

▶ Point to and describe each child standing in line. Say: *I see a boy wearing a red and blue shirt. He is first in line. He is in front of a girl who has straight blonde hair.*

▶ Repeat for other children in line. Use the Math Vocabulary words to describe their positions.

▶ Ask children to choose a child in line. Guide them in describing the child's position, using the vocabulary words.

▶ Place the card in the Math Center. Children can use the picture as a reference for describing the positions of people and things in the classroom.

Make It Easier Ask a small group of children to line up. Children can describe where they are in line using the vocabulary words. Or, another group can describe the order of the children. Have children rearrange themselves and repeat.

Make It Harder Challenge children to arrange group members in a line by asking them to take certain positions. For example, they can say: *Please stand first in line. Please stand in front of Tim.* Continue by having other children rearrange the group.

Lesson Tips

■ Ask three or four children to stand in a line. Invite them to describe their own position in the line. Then ask others to describe the positions of their classmates. Repeat with different groups and arrangements.

■ Provide children with many opportunities to describe the relative positions of classroom objects and the position of children or toy animals in a line. Frequent practice will help them to understand and use the vocabulary for position words with greater accuracy and ease.

Home Connection

Post Math Card 5 on your family communication board so that families know what children are learning about position words. Encourage them to help children use these words to describe the position of things at home and their position when standing in line at a store.

MATH CONCEPT CARD
6
Position Words

Who is inside the playhouse? Who is outside?

6

Who is inside the playhouse? Who is outside?

Geometry/ Spatial Sense
• understands and describes position

Math Vocabulary
down
far
inside
near
outside
up

Position Words

▶ Point to and describe the location of the children.

▶ Point to one of the girls. Say: **This girl is *inside* the playhouse.** Repeat for the other children and the chair. Use the vocabulary words to describe their positions.

▶ Ask children to choose someone or something in the picture. Guide them in describing the position, using the vocabulary words.

▶ Place the card in the Math Center. Children can describe the positions of people and things on the card as well as in the classroom.

Make It Easier Display several classroom toys. Use the Math Vocabulary words to describe their positions. Ask children to repeat the sentences after you. Then describe the children on the Math Card using the vocabulary words. Ask children to point to the child you describe.

Make It Harder Challenge the group to guess an item you are thinking of by providing clues about its position. For example, say: *I am thinking of something that is (outside) the box.* Whoever guesses the object can think of the next item.

Lesson Tips

■ Reduce the number of factors in the positions children describe by having a child sit down inside a box, outside the box, near the box, and far from the box. Describe each position. Repeat with an object that is in the box, out of the box, and near and far from the box.

Home Connection

Post Math Card 6 on your family communication board so that families know what children are learning about position words. Encourage them to help children use these words to describe things at home or when they are on walks in their community.

What is under the bridge? What is on the bridge?

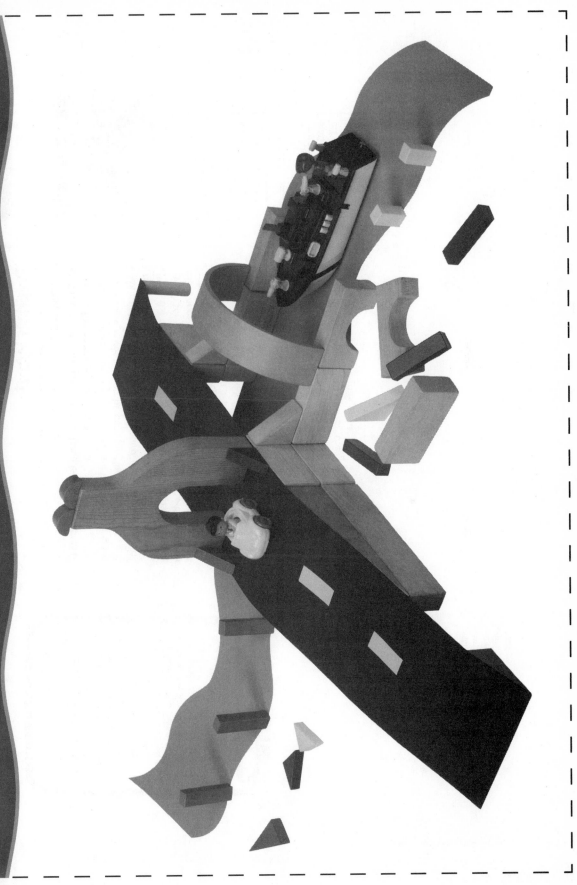

Position Words

▶ Point to and name the road, bridge, river, car, and boat in the photograph.

▶ Point to the bridge and river. Say: **There is a river under the bridge. The bridge goes over the river.**

▶ Next, describe the position of the car and the boat, using the vocabulary words to describe each position.

▶ Ask children the questions on the card. Guide them in using the vocabulary words to answer the questions.

▶ Place the card in the Math Center. Children can use the photograph for describing the positions of people and things in the classroom, and of objects in picture books and posters.

Make It Easier Build a scene similar to the one on the card, using blocks, construction paper, and vehicles from the block area. Place a toy boat under the bridge and a toy car on the bridge. Place other toy vehicles on and off the road and bridge. Ask children to choose one vehicle and describe where it is.

Make It Harder Challenge children to direct a partner in building a scene like the one on the card. Encourage them to use the Math Vocabulary to describe where each item should go. Start them off with examples, such as: *Make a river. Build a bridge over the river. Place a car on the bridge.* Partners can trade roles and build another scene.

LEARNING GOALS

Geometry/ Spatial Sense
• understands and describes positions

Math Vocabulary
off
on
over
under

Lesson Tips

■ Ask questions about the scene, for example: *Where is the boat? Where is the river?* Have children answer the questions using complete sentences: *The river is under the bridge.*

■ Describe the positions of objects in the classroom. Model using the words *off, on, over,* and *under* while the children play outside. Frequent exposure will help children to understand and use the vocabulary for position words with greater accuracy and ease.

Home Connection

Post Math Card 7 on your family communication board so that families know what children are learning about position words. Encourage them to help children use these words to describe things at home or when playing at a playground.

MATH CONCEPT CARD

8

Comparing Groups

Compare the groups.

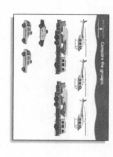

LEARNING GOALS

Numbers
- compares numbers of objects
- indicates the same number, more, or fewer

Math Vocabulary

equal
fewer
more
same number

Comparing Groups

▶ Point to and name the objects in each group.

▶ Point to the group of helicopters. Say: **Let's count the helicopters. One, two three. There are three helicopters.**

▶ Repeat, counting the fire trucks.

▶ Help children compare the number of helicopters and fire trucks. Ask: **Which group has more, the helicopters or fire trucks? Three is more than two. Yes, there are more helicopters than fire trucks.**

▶ Ask: **Is there another way to tell which group has more?** Children may suggest that you can match the helicopters and the fire trucks one to one.

▶ Repeat, comparing other groups. Help children use the vocabulary words to answer the questions on the front of the card. Tell children that *equal* also means the *same number*.

▶ Place the card in the Math Center. Ask children to compare other groups of objects in the classroom using the vocabulary *equal*, *fewer*, *more*, and *same number*.

Make It Easier Gather two types of objects such as markers and crayons. Form one group with two markers and a second group with three crayons. Demonstrate comparing the groups using one-to-one correspondence. Ask children to physically match the objects in the two sets. Ask: **Are there as many markers as there are crayons? No, there are** *fewer* **markers than crayons. There are** *more* **crayons than markers.**

Make It Harder Challenge children to compare groups that are close in number and to include a number in their comparison statements. For example, say: *There are two more helicopters than police cars.*

Lesson Tips

■ For each sentence used to compare groups, offer a restatement using opposite pairs of words from the Math Vocabulary. For example, say: *There are more helicopters than fire trucks. There are fewer fire trucks than helicopters.* After a few examples, start the second sentence and pause for children to complete it.

■ Use everyday experiences to compare quantity. For example, when passing out markers to a small group, you can ask: *Do you think we have enough markers so that each child has one marker? Do you think we have too many and we will have some left over?* Distribute the markers, discuss the results, and then state the comparison.

Home Connection

Post Math Card 8 on your family communication board so that families know what children are learning about comparing amounts. Encourage them to help children practice comparing groups of objects at home.

How many do you see? 1 or 2?

Numbers: One and Two

▶ Discuss the photograph with children. Read the questions on the card. Guide children to see that there are two children, *one hat,* and *two pigtails.*

▶ Ask other questions, such as: *How many eyes does the girl have? Does the boy have one or two noses?* Have children point to the numeral on the card that goes with the answer.

▶ Place the card in the Math Center. Children can use the photograph for counting activities. Encourage them count other groups of one or two objects such as counters, cubes, and other manipulatives in the classroom.

Make It Easier Play "1 Clap, 2 Claps." Call out one or two in random order and clap once or twice to match the number. Then have children clap once or twice to match for one and two. Finally, clap once or twice randomly and have children call out one or two to match.

Make It Harder Supply pairs with two markers and two crayons. One partner calls out a number of objects (for example: *two markers*). The other partner counts the correct number of items, says the total, and points to the corresponding numeral on the card. Partners switch roles and repeat the activity.

Lesson Tips

■ Make numeral cards 1 and 2. Place a group of objects in the middle of the table. Call out a number and have each child take that number of objects. Ask a child to select a numeral card that matches the number you named. Repeat the activity several times. Place the objects and numeral cards in the Math Center.

■ Throughout the lesson, have children show one and two fingers when amounts are counted and used to describe a number of objects.

■ Invite children to take turns gently tapping once or twice on their partner's back and having the partner name the number.

■ Involve children in counting out groups of objects and reading numerals 1 and 2 throughout the day. Frequent counting opportunities will help children increase their number concepts.

LEARNING GOALS

Numbers
- understands that numbers represent quantity
- builds sets of one and two
- counts to one and two
- matches groups of objects to numerals

Math Vocabulary
one
two

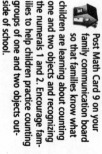

Home Connection

Post Math Card 9 on your family communication board so that families know what children are learning about counting one and two objects and recognizing the numerals 1 and 2. Encourage families to help children practice counting groups of one and two objects outside of school.

MATH CONCEPT CARD
10
Numbers: Three and Four

How many are there? 3 or 4?

Numbers: Three and Four

Numbers: Three and Four

▶ Point to and name the objects in the photograph.

▶ Read the questions on the card. Then point to and count the plates. Say: **One, two, three, four plates. There are *four* plates. Three plates are big and 1 plate is small. There are four plates in all.**

▶ Have children count the other objects in the photograph. Help them find sets of three and four. Have children point to the numeral on the card that goes with each answer.

▶ Place the card in the Math Center. Children can use the photograph for counting activities. Have them use counters, bears, or other concrete manipulatives to make groups of three or four objects.

Make It Easier Place a group of objects such as color tiles or bears in the middle of the table. Call out a number and show that number of objects. Have children match your set. Together count the group of objects. Help children understand that the number name of three or four applies not only to the last object counted, but also to the entire set.

Make It Harder Give each child a piece of chalk and ask children to stand at the board. Call out and display a number card from 1 to 4. Ask children to draw the number of tally marks equal to the number you say.

LEARNING GOALS

Numbers
- understands that numbers represent quantity
- counts to three and four
- builds sets of three and four
- matches groups of objects to numerals

Math Vocabulary
four
three

Lesson Tips

- Throughout the lesson, have children show three or four fingers on one hand, to match the number of objects being described.
- Guide children to understand that 3 counters is 1 more than 2 counters; and that 4 counters is 1 more than 3 counters.
- Use the floor number line and ask children to follow directions: Stand on 2. Move forward to 4. Move back to 1. Stand on 3. Move back 1. What number are you standing on now?
- Involve children in counting groups of objects and reading numerals 3 and 4 at Meeting Time or at snack time.

Home Connection

Post Math Card 10 on your family communication board so that families know what children are learning about the numbers three and four. Encourage them to help children practice counting groups of three and four things at home, in the grocery store, or when on a walk in their neighborhood.

MATH CONCEPT CARD
11
Number: Five

How many balls do you see? Count them.

5

How many balls do you see? Count them.

LEARNING GOALS

Numbers
- understands that numbers represent quantity
- counts to five
- builds sets of five
- matches groups of objects to numerals

Math Vocabulary
five

Number: Five

▶ Point to and discuss the balls in the photograph.

▶ Read the question on the card. Then point to the balls one at a time as you count them to answer the question. **Say: One, two, three, four, five balls. There are five balls.** Have children point to the numeral that goes with the answer.

▶ Help children count the balls again. Point out that 5 can be made up of 3 and 2.

▶ Place the card in the Math Center. Children can use the photograph for counting. Help them count other groups of five using counters, blocks, tiles, or manipulatives in your classroom.

Make It Easier Display a set of five markers. Together count the set. Show that there is one-to-one correspondence between each number name and the object in the set. When counting the set of five markers, the child points to the markers, in turn, while saying, one, two, three, four, five.

Make It Harder Play "I Spy." Find examples of groups of five objects around the classroom. **Say: I spy five (red markers).** Have children find the objects and count them out.

Lesson Tips

■ Have children use five fingers on one hand to check their counting. Help them see that they could also use 1 finger on one hand and 4 fingers on the other hand to show 5 fingers. Guide them to see other ways to show 5 fingers.

■ Invite children to clap five times every time they hear the word *five.*

■ Review reading numerals 1–5 with children. Display numeral cards 1–5. Ask a child to select a card and say the number. Then have other children build a set with that number. Repeat so that children can review building other sets and recognizing the numerals 1, 2, 3, 4, and 5.

Home Connection

Post Math Card 11 on your family communication board so that families know what children are learning about counting five objects and recognizing the numeral 5. Encourage them to help children practice counting groups of five things at home when helping with family chores such as folding laundry or setting the table.

How many do you see? Count them.

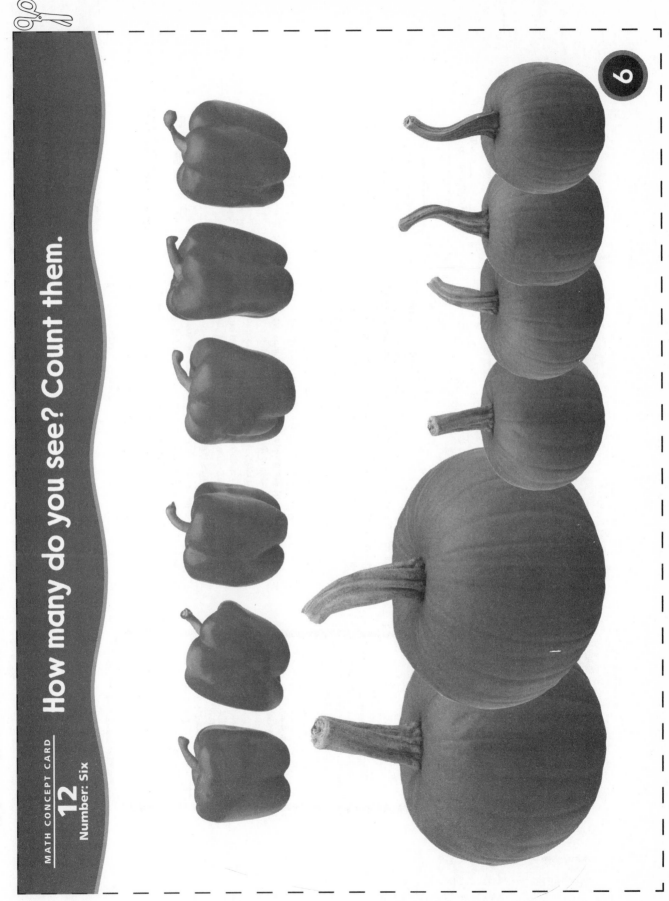

6

LEARNING GOALS

Numbers
- understands that numbers represent quantity
- builds sets of six
- counts to six
- matches groups of objects to numerals

Math Vocabulary
six

Number: Six

▶ Point to and discuss the items in the picture.

▶ Read the question on the card. Then point to the peppers in order as you model counting them. Say: **One, two, three, four, five, six peppers. There are six peppers. How many are red? How many are green?**

▶ Next, point to and read the numeral 6 on the front of the card. Say: **This is the number 6. There are six peppers. We can write the number 6 for the six peppers.**

▶ Help children count the pumpkins. Say: **One, two, three, four, five, six pumpkins. How many pumpkins are there in all? How many are small? How many pumpkins are big? How many are small?**

▶ Place the card in the Math Center. Children can use the picture to practice counting. Encourage them count other groups of six using counters, tiles, or other manipulatives.

Make It Easier Guide the group in counting from 1 to 6 while taking six steps, clapping six times, or hopping six hops. Ask different children to lead the counting on another round.

Make It Harder Challenge children to find examples of a group of six items. Children can count out the items in their group to show that there are six.

Lesson Tips

- Have children hold out the five fingers on one hand, and one finger on the other hand, to show six. Have them show 6 another way such as 4 and 2, 3 and 3, 2 and 4.

- Place a group of objects in the middle of a table. Put the numeral cards 5 and 6 next to the objects. Ask children to make a set of 6. Ask a child to select the numeral card that matches the groups of 6.

- Involve children in counting items and reading numerals often. At snack time encourage children to count the number of items such as crackers, juice cups, or napkins. Children can also count the number of children sitting at a table and select a numeral card that shows that number.

Home Connection

Post Math Card 12 on your family communication board so that families know what children are learning about the number six. Encourage them to help children practice counting groups of six things at home or when outside.

How many lunch bags do you see? Count them.

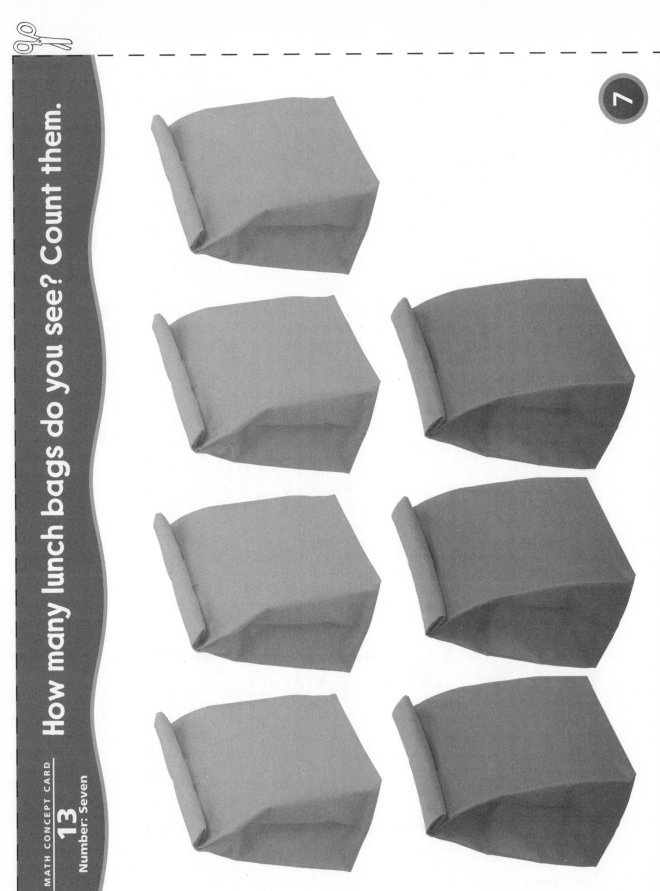

How many lunch bags do you see? Count them.

Number: Seven

▶ Point to and name the items in the photograph.

▶ Read the question on the card. Then point to the lunch bags one at a time to model how to count them. Say: **One, two, three, four, five, six, seven lunch bags. There are seven lunch bags.**

▶ Point to and read the numeral 7 on the front of the card. Say: **This is the number 7. There are seven lunch bags. We can write the number 7 for the seven lunch bags.**

▶ Help children to count the number of lunch bags. Ask: **How many yellow lunch bags are there? How many blue lunch bags? How many in all?**

▶ Place the card in the Math Center. Children can use the photograph to practice counting. Help them count other groups of seven using bears, counters, blocks, or other manipulatives in the classroom.

Make It Easier Ask children to listen as you tap on a table seven times. Repeat, having children count aloud as you tap.

Make It Harder Have children draw a group of seven objects. Invite them to share their pictures and count out the objects aloud.

LEARNING GOALS

Numbers
- understands that numbers represent quantity
- counts to seven
- builds sets of seven
- matches groups of objects to numerals

Math Vocabulary
seven

Lesson Tips
- Have children hold out five fingers on one hand and two fingers on the other hand to show seven. Ask then other hand to show seven fingers in other ways; for example 2 and 5, 1 and 6, and 1, 4 and 3, or 3 and 4.
- Ask children to count out seven blocks. Then have them make different block structures each with seven blocks. Have children describe the block buildings and count to verify the number of blocks in each structure. Point out how each block building may look different, but each block building still has seven blocks.
- Involve children in counting groups of objects throughout the day. Frequent application will help children to understand and use the Math Vocabulary with ease.

Home Connection

Post Math Card 13 on your family communication board so that families know what children are learning about the number seven. Encourage them to help children practice counting groups of seven things at home or when they are outside playing.

MATH CONCEPT CARD
14
Number: Eight

How many flowers do you see? Count them.

8

Number: Eight

How many flowers do you see? Count them.

LEARNING GOALS

Numbers
- understands that numbers represent quantity
- counts to eight
- builds sets of eight
- matches groups of objects to numerals

Math Vocabulary
eight

Number: Eight

▶ Point to and name the flowers in the photograph.

▶ Read the question on the card. Then point to the flowers one at a time as you model how to count them. Say: **One, two, three, four, five, six, seven, eight flowers. There are eight flowers.** Point out that eight flowers is one more than seven flowers.

▶ Point to and read the numeral 8 on the front of the card. Say: **This is the number 8. There are eight flowers. We write the number 8 to tell how many flowers there are.**

▶ Help children to count the number of flowers. Ask: **How many yellow flowers (daffodils) are there? How many red flowers (tulips) are there? How many in all?**

▶ Place the card in the Math Center. Children can use the photograph for counting. Help them count other groups of eight objects such as pennies or counters.

Make It Easier Guide the children in counting from one to eight while taking eight steps, clapping eight times, or hopping eight hops. Ask different children to lead the counting on another round.

Make It Harder Give pairs a group of eight objects. Ask one child to make a group of three to eight objects. Ask the other child to count the objects and add more, if necessary, to make a group of eight. Have children switch roles.

Lesson Tips

■ Have children hold out five fingers on one hand and three fingers on the other hand to show eight. Ask children to try other ways to show eight fingers.

■ Draw eight stars on a large piece of paper. Then have children place one cube on each of the stars. Ask: **Are there as many cubes as stars? How do you know?** Children may say that each cube matches up with a star. Or, children may count the number of cubes and count the number of stars and compare the number of each.

■ Involve children in counting groups of objects in daily classroom routines, for example, handing out supplies, snacks, or notes.

Home Connection

 Post Math Card 14 on your family communication board so that families know what children are learning about counting eight objects and recognizing the numeral 8. Encourage them to help children practice counting groups of eight objects outside of school.

Number: Eight

MATH CONCEPT CARD
15
Number: Nine

How many jackets do you see? Count them.

Number: Nine

Number: Nine

▶ Point to and describe the jackets in the picture.

▶ Read the question on the card. Then point to the jackets one at a time as you model how to count them. Say: **One, two, three, four, five, six, seven, eight, nine. I see nine winter jackets.**

▶ Point to and read the numeral 9 on the front of the card. Say: **This is the number 9. There are nine jackets. We write the number 9 to tell how many jackets there are.**

▶ Help children to count the number of jackets. Guide children to see that nine is one more than eight.

▶ Place the card in the Math Center. Children can use the picture to practice counting. Help them to count other groups of nine objects such as tiles or bears.

Make It Easier Have pairs make a tower using nine blocks. Ask them to count out the blocks together.

Make It Harder Challenge children to make sets of nine objects. Children should count out the items in their group to show that there are nine.

Lesson Tips

■ Have children hold out five fingers on one hand and four fingers on the other hand to show nine. Ask children to also show four fingers and five fingers.

■ Give pairs nine attribute blocks. Ask them to make a design or pattern using the blocks. Have them count the blocks in their design. Point out that the number of blocks does not change if the child changes the arrangement of the blocks. Also, if two children compare their block patterns each has 9 blocks, but the patterns may look very different.

■ Involve children in counting out groups of objects frequently. Children need numerous experiences to match, compare, order, and describe sets to develop conservation of number.

Home Connection

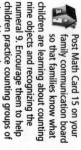

Post Math Card 15 on your family communication board so that families know what children are learning about counting nine objects and recognizing the numeral 9. Encourage them to help children practice counting groups of nine objects at home.

LEARNING GOALS

Numbers
- understands that numbers represent quantity
- counts to nine
- builds sets of nine
- matches groups of objects to numerals

Math Vocabulary
nine

MATH CONCEPT CARD
16
Number: Ten

How many foods do you see? Count them.

10

Number: Ten

Number: Ten

▸ Point to and name the different foods in the photograph.

▸ Read the question on the card. Then point to the foods one at a time as you model how to count them. Say: **One, two, three, four, five, six, seven, eight, nine, ten. I see ten kinds of food.**

▸ Point to and read the numeral 10 on the front of the card. Say: **This is the number 10. There are ten kinds of foods on the card. We write the number 10 to tell how many foods there are.**

▸ Help children count the number of foods. Help them choose a beginning point and a method of pointing and counting to make sure they count all the foods. Guide them to see that 10 is one more than 9.

▸ Place the card in the Math Center. Children can use the photograph to practice counting. Help children count other groups of ten objects such as pennies or beans.

Make It Easier Give children counting bears and a ten-frame workmat. Tell stories that require children to create sets, and then add 1 more bear or remove 1 bear. For example, say: **There were nine bears looking for honey.** (Children place nine bears on their mats.) **One more bear joined them.** (Children place one more bear on their mats.) **How many bears are looking for honey now?** Guide children to say, **9 and 1 more is 10. 9, 10. That's right, there are ten bears.** Have children clear their mats and then continue with other stories.

Make It Harder Show various groups of objects of different quantities. Ask: **Which two groups make ten?** Have children count the groups and tell how they can make ten. For example: A group of two and a group of eight make a group of ten.

Learning Goals

Numbers
• understands that numbers represent quantity
• counts to ten
• builds sets of ten
• matches groups of objects to numerals

Math Vocabulary
ten

Lesson Tips

■ Invite children to name their favorite food, and to draw ten of that food, or ten servings of it. Have them label the foods with numerals 1–10.

■ Have children hold out the fingers on both hands. Have them count the five fingers on one hand, and then continue counting up to ten on the other hand.

■ You can make ten-frame counting mats by taking off two sections of an egg carton.

Home Connection

Post Math Card 16 on your family communication board so that families know what children are learning about counting ten objects. Encourage parents to help children practice counting groups of ten things at home.

How many beach balls do you see?

0 1 2 3 4

How many toucan balls do you see?

0 1 2 3 4

Number: Zero

▶ Point to and name the different kinds of objects in the picture. Then count the number in each set. Ask: **How many rakes do you see? One, two, three, four. I see four rakes.** Continue with the kites, mittens, and sand pail.

▶ Read the question on the card. Help children to understand that there are no beach balls shown. Say: **There are no beach balls. Zero is the number you say when there are none.**

▶ Point to and read the numeral 0 on the front of the card. Say: **This is the number zero. There are zero beach balls. We write the number 0 to tell that there are no beach balls.**

▶ Modify the question to ask about other things that are not in the picture. For example, ask: **How many (sleds) do you see?** zero.

▶ Place the card in the Math Center to remind children about zero.

Make It Easier

Have five children sit down in a row. Then ask four children to stand up. Ask: **How many children are sitting?** When children answer one, ask the remaining child to stand up. Ask: **How many are left sitting now? That's right, zero children are sitting now.** Reinforce that zero means *not any or none.*

Make It Harder

Write *0* at the top of one sheet of paper and *5* at the top of the other sheet. Challenge children to display two groups of items to show the number at the top of each sheet of paper. For example, children might show five markers on a sheet of paper labeled *5,* and zero markers on a sheet of paper labeled *0.*

LEARNING GOALS

Numbers
• understands that numbers represent quantity
• recognizes and names examples of zero
• matches groups of objects to numerals

Math Vocabulary
zero

Lesson Tips

■ When answering the question, children may reply *not any or no beach balls.* Explain that zero is the special number used to mean *not any or none.* Guide them in answering: *There are not any or zero beach balls.*

■ Have children hold up five fingers on one hand. Lead them in counting down from five to zero, putting a finger down each time to match the count.

■ Give each child two workmats. Place blue and red colored tiles in the middle of a table. Ask children to show a set of blue tiles from 1 to 10 on one mat. Then ask them to show a set of 0 red tiles on their other mat. Ask: **How many red tiles are there?** Repeat, having children compare different sets with zero.

Home Connection

Post Math Card 17 on your family communication board so that families know what children are learning about zero. Encourage them to help children practice counting groups of things at home and noting when there is *zero* or *not any* of an object they are discussing.

Which dog is first? Which dog is third?

LEARNING GOALS

Numbers
- uses ordinal numbers *first* to *fifth* to show position

Math Vocabulary
first
second
third
fourth
fifth

Position Words: Ordinals

▶ Point to and describe each dog by color.

▶ Point to the first dog on the left. Say: I see a brown and **white dog. It is the *first dog* in line.**

▶ Repeat for other dogs. Use the Math Vocabulary to describe the order of the dogs.

▶ Ask children to choose a dog. Guide them to describe the dog's position, using the vocabulary words.

▶ Place the card in the Math Center. Children can use the photograph to help them remember the vocabulary. Name the position, or order, of people and things in the classroom to provide more experience for children to name the ordinal number words for first through fifth.

Make It Easier Line up five toy animals. Reinforce the connection between the ordinal and cardinal numbers. First, point to and count the animals, one, two, three, four, five. Then point to each one as you say *first, second, third, fourth, fifth*. Repeat, asking children to join you by saying the ordinal number words.

Make It Harder Challenge children to arrange group members in a line. Ask them to describe the ordinal position; for example, *Carlos is first, Joe is second,* and so on. Continue by having other children rearrange the group and state the order of children.

Lesson Tips

- Arrange five children in a line facing the door. Point to each child as you say *first, second, third, fourth, fifth*. Next, invite them to tell their own position. Then ask questions of the whole group: *Who is third? Who is second?* Repeat with other groups of five.

- As children line up for different activities, review ordinal numbers for the first five children in line. You can also review the ordinals to describe actions or steps in a process. Frequent practice will help children to understand and use the Math Vocabulary with greater ease.

Home Connection

 Post Math Card 18 on your family communication board so that families know what children are learning about order words. Encourage parents to help children use these words to describe their position in a checkout line.

What do you see?

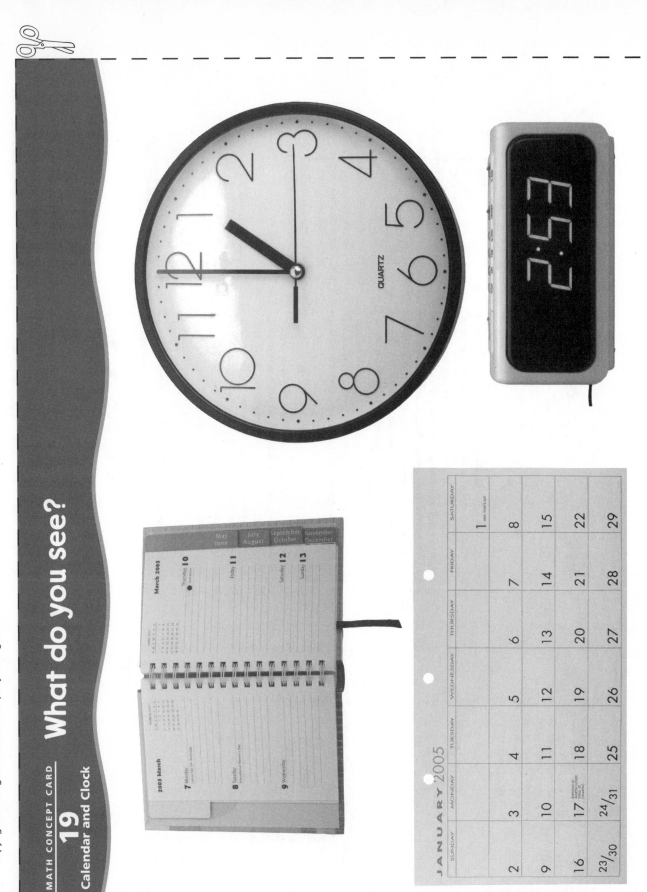

19

LEARNING GOALS

Time Concepts
- identifies use of a clock and calendar

Math Vocabulary
calendar
clock
day
date
month
time

Calendar and Clock

▶ Point to the two clocks. Say: These are both clocks. Clocks show people what time it is.

▶ Discuss the differences between the two clocks. Point to the analog clock. Say: **The hands on this clock point to numbers to tell what time it is.** Point to the digital clock. Say: **This clock is a digital clock. It tells time by just showing numbers.**

▶ Point to the calendar. Say: **This is a calendar. A calendar tells you what time of year it is. It tells you the month. It tells you the days of the week and the date for each day.** Point to the date book. Say: **A date book is a different kind of calendar that people write in. A date book helps people remember important things each day.**

▶ Ask children the questions on the card. Guide them to answer using the vocabulary words.

▶ Place the card in the Math Center. Children can use it to help identify other clocks and calendars in the classroom and around school.

Make It Easier Discuss with children the different times of the day. Talk about what they do in the morning, afternoon, and evening. Then discuss different times of the year. Talk about what they do during the different seasons. Help them understand that clocks and calendars help them know what time of day and year it is.

Make It Harder If children know the names of the days of the week, help them learn the names of the months of the year.

Lesson Tips

- Display a demonstration clock, or use the wall clock in the picture, and point to the numbers as children say them.

- Page through a monthly calendar with children, reciting the names of the months. Mention something special about each month. Point to and say the days of the week in order.

- Take every opportunity to identify the date and time with children. Frequent practice with clocks and calendars will help them to understand the use of these tools.

Home Connection

Post Math Card 19 on your family communication board so that families know what children are learning about the clock and calendar. Encourage families to use a calendar and clock to talk about the date and time with children at home.

Where is it warmer? Where is it colder?

LEARNING GOALS

Measurement
- compares temperature

Math Vocabulary

cold
colder
cool
cooler
hot
hotter
temperature
warmer

Comparing Temperature

▶ Point to the first picture and describe the weather and the clothes the girl is wearing. Say: It's snowing where this girl is. It must be winter. The temperature in winter is *colder* than in summer. It's cold outside, so the girl is wearing a coat, a headband, and mittens.

▶ Point to the second picture and describe it in a similar way. Say: **The temperature is much *warmer* in this picture. It's *hotter* in the summer than in the winter. That's why the boy is wearing shorts and a t-shirt.**

▶ Have children answer the questions on the card. Guide them in using the vocabulary words to describe and compare the weather in each picture.

▶ Place the card in the Math Center. Children can use the picture for comparing the temperature in other situations, such as in stories and in the daily weather.

Make It Easier Ask children to tell if the weather in each picture is *hot* or *cold*. Have them describe the features in the picture that helped them reach their decision.

Make It Harder Ask children to find picture books that show children or animals playing in warm weather and in colder weather. Invite them to share the pictures, describing and comparing the pictures using the vocabulary words.

Lesson Tips

- Display pictures where the temperature or season is obvious. Ask children to sort the pictures into two piles, *warmer* and *cooler*.
- Have children cut out magazine pictures that show weather when the temperature is hot or cold. Have them compare the pictures.
- Discuss the daily weather and the weather in stories and books you read together. Frequent exposure will help children to understand and use the Math Vocabulary with greater ease.

Home Connection

Post Math Card 20 on your family communication board so that families know what children are learning about comparing temperature. Encourage families to help children talk about weather and how it changes.

What comes next?

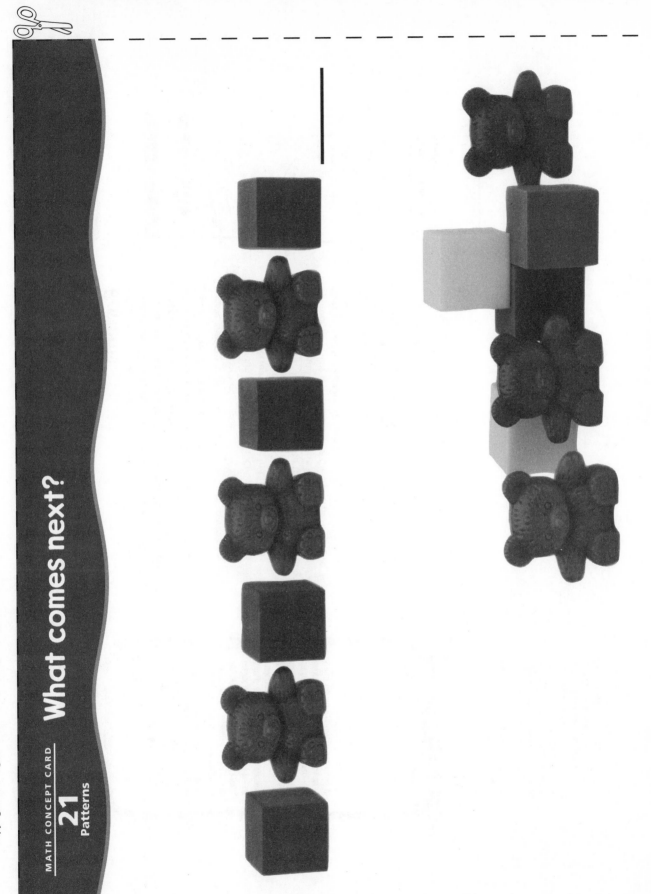

MATH CONCEPT CARD

21

LEARNING GOALS

Patterns
- describes simple patterns
- predicts and extends patterns

Math Vocabulary
order
pattern
repeat

Patterns

▸ Point to the row of cubes and bears and say: **Look at the cubes and bears. First, there's a cube, then a bear, then a cube, then a bear, and then a cube again. The *order repeats* again and again. This is called a *pattern*.**

▸ Ask: **What comes next, a cube or a bear?** Discuss children's suggestions. **Yes, a bear comes next!**

▸ Have children extend the pattern. Ask them to describe the pattern with each addition.

▸ Place the card in the Math Center. Children can use it to help identify and create other patterns in the classroom and around school.

Make It Easier Have five children form a line, alternating between boys and girls. Go down the line, saying *boy* or *girl* as appropriate. Have children describe the pattern. Then have them extend the pattern, deciding if a boy or girl should come next.

Make It Harder Have children work in pairs to create their own patterns with cubes, bears or other manipulatives. Then have them challenge each other to extend the patterns they make.

Lesson Tips

- Display similar AB patterns using other sets of objects, such as markers and crayons, or blocks and balls. Have children describe the patterns and predict which item comes next.

- Describe simple, concrete patterns in the room. For example, point out a zebra's stripes on a poster or colored bricks in the wall. Show how these things are in an order that repeats, making a pattern.

- Provide children with many opportunities to make, describe, and extend patterns in the classroom. Frequent exposure will help them to understand the concepts and vocabulary of pattern recognition.

Home Connection

Post Math Card 21 on your family communication board so that families know what children are learning about patterns. Encourage families to find and name patterns at home, and to work together with their child to predict the next item in a pattern.

Where do you see a number? What does it tell you?

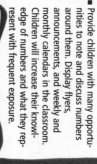

Numbers All Around

▶ Explain that the picture shows a school fair. Encourage children to describe the activities they see.

▶ Read the questions on the card. Point to the banner and say: I see a *number* here. It's 22. **The sign says Saturday, October 22. That *number* tells me when the school fair takes place. It tells me the *date*.**

▶ Ask children to find other numbers in the picture. Help them figure out what information the number tells them. Guide children in using the Math Vocabulary to tell what the numbers mean.

▶ Place the card in the Math Center. Children can use it to help identify other numbers in the classroom and around school.

Make It Easier Point to familiar places in the classroom where there are numbers, such as on a clock or a calendar. Have children point to the numbers, and then talk about what the numbers mean.

Make It Harder Ask children to go on a number hunt in the classroom. Each time a child finds a number, involve the group in identifying and determining what it tells. Items with numbers might include a calendar, clock, cubbies, posters, flyers, maps, schedules.

LEARNING GOALS

Numbers and Operations
• recognizes numbers in the environment

Math Vocabulary
date
number
price
time

Lesson Tips

▪ Point out the cents (¢) symbol and explain what it means.

▪ To help children determine what a number stands for, ask simple questions. For example, point to the pretzels and ask: *How many cents do you need to buy a pretzel?*

▪ Provide children with many opportunities to note and discuss numbers around them. Display flyers, announcements, and weekly and monthly calendars in the classroom. Children will increase their knowledge of numbers and what they represent with frequent exposure.

Home Connection

Post Math Card 22 on your family communication board so that families know what children are learning about numbers all around them. Encourage families to notice and discuss numbers they see with children at home and in their travels and activities.

Which is longer, the marker or the paintbrush?

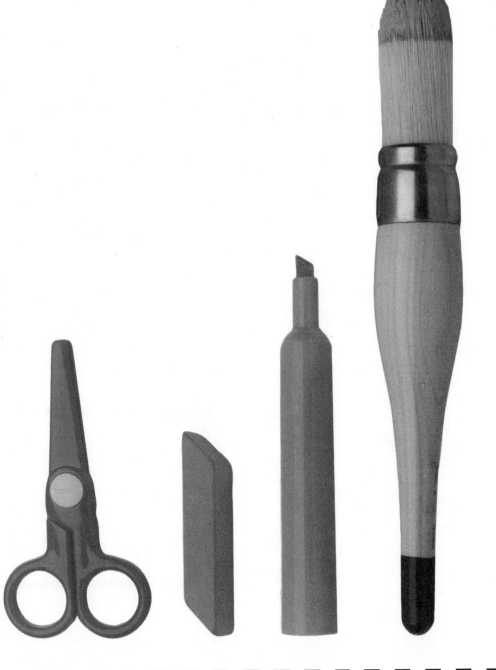

LEARNING GOALS

Measurement
- compares length of objects

Math Vocabulary
about the same
length
longer
longer than
shorter
shorter than
taller
taller than

Comparing Lengths

▶ Cover all but the marker on the card. Hold up a pencil or an object longer than the marker, and say: **This (pencil) is longer than the marker.** Show how you compare the lengths by lining up the ends of the objects.

▶ Repeat with a crayon or an object shorter than the marker. Say: **This (crayon) is shorter than the marker.**

▶ Have children name classroom objects that are *longer than,* *shorter than,* and *about the same length* as the marker. Verify children's suggestions by holding the objects next to the marker.

▶ Continue by comparing the length of the marker and the paintbrush. Guide children to use the vocabulary words to answer the question on the card.

▶ On Day 4, use the card to compare the height of different objects using the words *taller than* and *shorter than.*

▶ Place the card in the Math Center. Children can compare the length of objects with those pictured on the card.

Make It Easier
Children can compare objects that vary greatly in length. Have them run their fingers along the length of each object so they can combine tactile clues with the visual ones.

Make It Harder
Challenge children to find four objects: two *longer than* and two *shorter than* the paintbrush. Have children share their findings using the Math Vocabulary for comparing.

Lesson Tips

■ Demonstrate lining up objects to compare length. Say: **I put the ends of the paintbrush and the marker on this line. Now I can compare the lengths. Look how far the paintbrush sticks out past the marker. This means that the paintbrush is *longer than* the marker. The marker is *shorter than* the paintbrush.**

■ If children have difficulty lining up the ends of objects when comparing length, place a piece of tape on a table in the Math Center. Children can line up the ends of the objects on the tape when they compare the length of them.

■ Use the phrases *longer than* and *shorter than* frequently when talking about the lengths of objects with children, both during the lesson and throughout the day.

Home Connection

Post Math Card 23 on your family communication board so that families know what children are learning about comparing lengths. Encourage families to notice and discuss lengths of objects with children at home, at the grocery or hardware store, or at the playground.

24
Comparing Weight

Which is heavier? Which is lighter?

Comparing Weight

▶ Point out the wheelbarrow with three bricks and say: **Bricks weigh a lot. They are heavy.** Pantomime lifting the wheelbarrow with three bricks.

▶ Repeat for the wheelbarrow with more bricks and say: **There are even more bricks in this wheelbarrow. This wheelbarrow is *heavier than* the other wheelbarrow. The wheelbarrow with three bricks is *lighter than* this one.**

▶ Using blocks or books of different weights, continue the discussion. Have children pick up one object and talk about how heavy it is. Ask a child to pick up another object and talk about how heavy it is. Ask: **Which object is *heavier?* Which object is *lighter?*** Verify children's suggestions by comparing the weight of the objects in your hands. Invite others to weigh them similarly.

▶ Repeat with other objects. Guide children to use the vocabulary words as they decide which object is heavier and which object is lighter; for example, **The block is *heavier than the* marker. The marker is *lighter than the* block.**

▶ Place the card in the Math Center. Children can use the two wheelbarrows of bricks as a reminder of what is heavier and what is lighter.

Make It Easier Children can compare objects that vary greatly in weight. Have children weigh items in their hands to decide which is heavier and which is lighter.

Make It Harder Challenge children to find four objects: two *heavier than* and two *lighter than* an object such as a block. Have children share their findings. Encourage others to verify the findings and to express the comparisons using the Math Vocabulary.

Lesson Tips

- Use blocks, books, or other objects to show how weight increases as you add more objects. Start with three blocks. Then have children compare the weight of three blocks to the weight of four blocks and then five blocks.

- Use a similar procedure to explore *lighter than*. Start with five blocks and reduce the number to show how weight decreases as you take away objects.

- Children can predict which of two objects is heavier. Then they can verify their predictions using the bucket balance.

- Use the phrases *heavier than* and *lighter than* frequently when talking with children, both during the lesson and throughout the day.

Home Connection

Post Math Card 24 on your family communication board so that families know what children are learning about comparing weight. Encourage families to observe and discuss the weight of objects with children at home, in the produce section of a market, and when taking a walk in their neighborhood.

LEARNING GOALS

Measurement
- compares weight of objects

Math Vocabulary
heavy
heavier than
light
lighter than

Which holds more? Which holds less?

MATH CONCEPT CARD

25

LEARNING GOALS

Measurement
• explores capacity

Math Vocabulary
less
more

Comparing Capacity

▶ Point out the glass of juice and the pitcher of juice as you say: **This glass holds a little juice. This pitcher holds a lot of juice.**

▶ Ask the questions on the card and model using the vocabulary words to answer them. For example, say: **The pitcher holds more juice than the glass. The glass holds *less* juice than the pitcher.**

▶ Ask children to name and tell what they know about other the containers in the picture. Help children identify and describe the measuring cups and bowls as needed.

▶ Point to two of the pictured containers. Ask: **Which holds *more*? Which holds *less*?** Guide children in using the vocabulary words to answer the questions

▶ Continue by having children compare the capacity of other pairs of containers. Children can tell which holds *more* and which holds *less.*

▶ Place the card in the Math Center. Children can compare containers that vary greatly in capacity. Have children select two containers and predict which holds more and which holds less. Ask them to describe what happens when they pour sand, water, or rice from the small container into the large container. Then have children tell what happens when they pour (sand) from the small container into the large container.

Make It Easier Children can compare the capacity of other classroom containers, using the card as a guide and the Math Vocabulary to describe their findings.

Make It Harder Ask partners to work at the sand or water table. Provide them with measuring cups and containers of different sizes. Children can select three containers and experiment to determine how to order them from the container that holds the least to the container that holds the most. Ask children to share their findings with others.

Lesson Tips

▪ Use containers like those pictured to provide hands-on demonstrations. Children can fill a container with sand, water, or other materials and then describe what happens when they pour the material into a smaller or larger container.

▪ Use the phrases *holds more* and *holds less* during sand and water play and in food preparation activities. This will reinforce the concept and the Math Vocabulary.

Home Connection

Post Math Card 25 on your family communication board so that families know what children are learning about comparing capacity. Encourage families to engage children in activities that involve measurement at home, such as cooking from a recipe, dividing portions, or feeding pets.

Comparing Capacity

What can you measure with each tool?

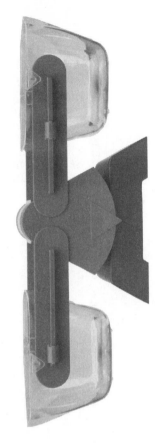

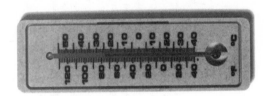

Tools for Measuring

Tools for Measuring

▶ Point to the cubes in the picture. Say: **We can use cubes to measure the length of an object.** Demonstrate using cubes to measure an object. Ask: **What else can we use to measure the length of this?** Measure the object using a different nonstandard unit.

▶ Point to the ruler and say: **This is a *ruler*. We can also use it to measure the length of an object. Carpenters use rulers to measure the length and height of things. Who else uses a ruler?**

▶ Display a classroom ruler and demonstrate measuring the length of an object. Measure different objects and compare their lengths.

▶ Guide children to identify each tool. Ask them to tell what they know about each tool. Talk about how they have used or seen people use the different tools.

▶ Place the card in the Math Center. Children can use it to help identify tools they need for measuring different things in the classroom and around school.

Make It Easier Focus on only one tool at a time. Give children the opportunity to use the tool to measure different materials in the classroom. For example, a measuring cup can be used in cooking or at the sand table. Talk about how each tool is used to measure.

Make It Harder Provide as many of the tools named in the Math Vocabulary as are available, along with objects and materials to measure. Guide children in using each tool, and then in grouping them by use. Say: **Which tools are used for measuring how long something is?** Ask children to think of other tools they could use to measure length, weight, amount, and temperature.

Lesson Tips

■ Display and demonstrate how to use the types of tools shown in the picture. Encourage children to use these tools during Center Time.

■ Provide children with opportunities to use standard and nonstandard tools for measuring. Frequent practice will help them to understand the use of these tools.

Home Connection

Post Math Card 26 on your family communication board so that families know what children are learning about tools for measuring. Encourage families to use different tools to measure the length of objects, weigh amounts, and find out temperatures with children at home.

LEARNING GOALS

Measurement
• uses standard and nonstandard tools to imitate measuring
• knows correct names for standard tools of measurement

Math Vocabulary
balance
measure
measuring tape
measuring cup
ruler
scale
thermometer

Tools for Measuring

What happens first? next? last?

Ordering Events

LEARNING GOALS

Time Concepts
- arranges time events in sequence

Math Vocabulary
first
next
last
order

Ordering Events

▸ Display the concept card. Ask children to describe what they see. Prompt them to talk about the house being built.

▸ Say: **These pictures show three different steps to make a house.** Point to each picture in order. Talk about the sequence. Use the terms *first*, *next*, and *last* when describing the sequence of building a house.

▸ Discuss with children why you need to build a house in order. For example, ask: **Do you build the roof before you build the walls? Why or why not?**

▸ Ask children to point to and tell about each picture. Encourage them to use the order vocabulary *first*, *next*, *last*.

▸ Place the card in the Math Center. Children can use it to help order steps when discussing the sequence of other activities in the classroom and around school.

Make It Easier Prepare a set of two drawings that show the sequence required for some simple classroom routine such as what the children do when they first arrive at school. Work with children to order the cards in the correct sequence. Then have children use the Math Vocabulary to tell the sequence.

Make It Harder Brainstorm with children simple three-step routines that they do before school in the morning. Distribute sheets of paper and have children draw the three steps. Children can tell others about their drawings using the Math Vocabulary.

Lesson Tips

- Make photocopies of the house pictures, Teacher's Resource Book p. 413. Cut the pictures apart. Mix up the pictures and have children put them in the correct order as they tell about the sequence for building a house.

- Lead children through a simple routine. For example, have children pretend to be putting on their socks and shoes. Describe the steps using the terms *first*, *next*, and *last*. Discuss what would happen if you didn't do things in the proper order.

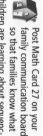

Home Connection

Post Math Card 27 on your family communication board so that families know what children are learning about sequencing events. Encourage parents to talk about the order of events when they read a story, plant a seed, or cook something at home.

Ordering Events

Which shows the whole? Which shows parts?

LEARNING GOALS

Numbers
- understands the concept of whole, parts, and parts that make a whole

Math Vocabulary
equal
part
whole

Whole and Parts

▶ Cover the pizza in the picture. Point to the whole sandwich and say: **This is a *whole* sandwich. What can we do if two people want to share it?**

▶ Point to the sandwich cut in half and say: **This sandwich is cut into two *parts*. Both parts are the same size. They are *equal*. Now two people can share it. Ask: Is there another way to make the sandwich into two parts?**

▶ Display the pizza and read the question on the card. Guide children in using the vocabulary words to answer the question.

▶ Place the card in the Math Center. Children can use it as a reference when dividing wholes into parts, and in general when sharing.

Make It Easier Distribute paper plates and markers or crayons. Children can decorate their plates like a pizza. Then lead children in "cutting" the pizza to show how to share it with two people. Children can then put the whole pizza back together again.

Make It Harder Challenge children to fold a square piece of paper into two parts. Then have them fold another square of paper to make four parts.

Lesson Tips

- Use colored tiles and modeling dough to provide hands-on demonstrations. For example, use four colored tiles to make a big square, and then divide it to show four parts. Children can also make a pie shape with modeling dough. Ask children to cut the pie into two parts or four parts. Talk about the equal parts.

- Draw a variety of shapes on the board. Demonstrate drawing a line to show how each whole can be divided into equal parts. Use one or more shapes to show how drawing the line elsewhere on the shape gives different-sized parts.

- Whenever sharing comes up in the classroom, use the opportunity to discuss and demonstrate dividing a whole into parts.

Home Connection

Post Math Card 28 on your family communication board so that families know what children are learning about wholes and parts of a whole. Encourage families to engage children in activities that involve sharing food items among two or more people, and to discuss how many equal parts are needed.

What money do you see?

Money

25 What money do you see?

LEARNING GOALS

Measurement
- identifies familiar U.S. coins
- recognizes that different coins have different values

Math Vocabulary
dime
dollar
nickel
penny
quarter

Money

▶ Display the picture and say: **Look at these coins and bills. These coins and bills are different kinds of money. We use money when we buy things. Each kind of money is worth a different amount of money.**

▶ Ask children to name and tell what they know about the money. Then point to the penny and say: **This coin is a penny. It is worth one cent.** Ask children to describe the penny. Say: **Yes, a penny is shiny. It is brown or copper colored.**

▶ Then point to the nickel and say: **This coin is a nickel. It is worth five cents, or five pennies.**

▶ Continue with the other coins and bills. Guide children in using the vocabulary words to identify each coin and bill.

▶ Place the card in the Math Center. Children can use it to help identify coins and bills.

Make It Easier Have pairs work with two different types of the manipulative coins, such as pennies and nickels. They can describe the size, shape, and color of each coin. Ask children to sort the coins by type.

Make It Harder Provide each partner with a handful of the manipulative pennies. Have them count out their pennies and compare the totals.

Lesson Tips

■ Display the manipulative coins for children to see and touch. Talk about the differences in the color and pictures on each coin.

■ As you discuss each coin, refer to the ones already introduced and explain how the values are related. For example, when identifying the dime as being worth ten cents, point out that it is the same as or equal to two nickels or ten pennies.

■ Children can use the play money in the Dramatic Play Center when playing store. They can also sort the coins in the Math Center. Frequent practice will help them to understand the names and values of the money.

Home Connection

Post Math Card 29 on your family communication board so that families know what children are learning about money. Encourage families to involve their children in counting out money for purchases or savings. Suggest that children start a piggy bank at home. Families can count pennies together.

MATH CONCEPT CARD

30
Symmetry

Do both parts match?

Symmetry

Do both parts match?

LEARNING GOALS

Geometry
- demonstrates an awareness of symmetry

Math Vocabulary
match
symmetry

Symmetry

▶ Use a card or sheet of paper to cover one wing of a butterfly. Say: **Look at the design on this butterfly wing.** Point out a few specific features, such as spots, swirls, and color patterns.

▶ Uncover the hidden wing, saying: **This wing matches the other one. It looks just like it. See the same (spot). The design is the same on both parts. This is called symmetry.** Point back and forth to show children the matching features.

▶ Read the sentence on the card. Examine the other insects with children. Hold up a mirror on the line of symmetry and ask children to name the matching parts.

▶ Place the card in the Math Center. Children can use it to help them identify symmetry in other objects in the classroom as well as in books and pictures.

Make It Easier Sketch a few shapes on the board. Work with children to place the mirror so they can see each matching part. Ask: **How do the two sides match?** Have children explain how each shape shows symmetry.

Make It Harder Challenge children to draw a picture that has symmetry, such as a house, heart, or circle. Encourage children to fold or draw a line on their paper so that they can draw one half on each side.

Lesson Tips

- To help children see the two different sides of the insects, hold a piece of string across the middle of each one.

- Show pictures of objects that do not show symmetry. Compare them with objects that show symmetry.

- Demonstrate how to make butterfly wings that match by cutting the shape out from a folded sheet of paper. Have children paint several spots or designs on one side of the paper. Then have them refold the paper and press the sides together. When children unfold their papers, they'll see how they painted symmetrical wings.

- Throughout the day, point out how two sides of appropriate things match, or show symmetry.

Home Connection

Post Math Card 30 on your family communication board so that families know what children are learning about symmetry. Encourage families to discuss objects that have matching sides with children at home, such as fruit and vegetables cut down the middle, or nuts cracked open in their shells.

MATH CONCEPT CARD
31
Problem Solving

How many birds are there in all?

Problem Solving

▸ Point to the feeder and ask: *How many birds are at the bird feeder?* Count the birds together. Say, Yes, there are three **birds. One, two, three birds.**

▸ Point to the bird flying toward the feeder and say: *How many more birds are flying to the feeder?* Count the one bird with children.

▸ Ask: *Now how many birds are there in all?* Count all four birds with children. Then say: **Yes, there are four birds!**

▸ Repeat, asking the question on the card. Call on children to point to the birds as they count them. Guide children to use the vocabulary words to tell about the problem.

▸ Place the card in the Math Center. Children can use it to help explore simple addition problems.

Make It Easier Tell combining stories for children to illustrate with counters such as teddy bears. Say: **Here are two teddy bears going for a walk. One more bear comes. Combine the bears. How many bears do you have now? Yes, one, two, three. There are three bears!** Continue with other stories for children to show and solve.

Make It Harder Give each child or small group a different number of counters, such as colored cubes. Ask them to count their cubes. Then add a cube to each child's set, asking them to count how many cubes they have now. Continue adding one cube at a time, and ask children to tell the total each time.

Lesson Tips

■ Point to each bird in the picture as children count. This concrete visual will help children understand the concept of one-to-one correspondence.

■ Use blocks or other manipulatives to represent the birds in the problem. Have children use the blocks to show how many birds are on the feeder at first, how many join the group, and then how many there are in all.

■ Provide children with many opportunities to solve simple combining (addition) problems in the classroom. Frequent usage will help them to understand the concepts and vocabulary used when telling combining stories.

Home Connection

Post Math Card 31 on your family communication board so that families know what children are learning to problem solve addition stories. Encourage families to work together with their child to solve similar problems at home, such as how many boxes of cereal are on the shelf before and after grocery shopping.

LEARNING GOALS

Numbers and Operations
• begins to combine and separate
• recognizes when a group is increased by one

Problem Solving
• explores and solves simple problems

Math Vocabulary
how many
in all

How many players are left?

LEARNING GOALS

Numbers and Operations
- begins to combine and separate
- recognizes when a group is decreased by one

Problem Solving
- explores and solves simple problems

Math Vocabulary
how many
left

Problem Solving

▶ Point to the children and ask: **How many children are playing soccer?** Count the children. Say: **Yes, there are four children, one, two, three, four children.**

▶ Point to the player who is leaving and ask: **How many players walk away?** Count the one player with children.

▶ **Now how many players are *left*?** Cover the player leaving with your hand. Then count the players who are left. Say: **One, two, three. There are three soccer players *left*.**

▶ Repeat, asking the question on the card. Call on children to point to the players as others count during each step. Help children use the vocabulary words to tell about the problem.

▶ Place the card in the Math Center. Children can use it to help explore simple subtraction problems.

Make It Easier Invite five children to stand up in front of the group. Have them count one-by-one. Then ask one child to sit down. Ask: **How many children sat down? How many children are left?** Count with the group to answer the questions. Repeat a few times.

Make It Harder Give each child or small group a different number of color cubes. Ask them to count their cubes. Then remove one cube from each child's set. Ask children to count how many cubes they have now. Repeat the activity, removing one cube again, and then two cubes.

Lesson Tips

- On the board, sketch the field with four players on it. Then erase the one player to show what happens when one player leaves. This concrete visual will help children understand the concepts of how many players are "left."

- Use blocks or other manipulatives to represent the players in the problem. Have children use the blocks to show how many players are on the field at first, how many walk away, and how many are left.

- Provide children with many opportunities to observe and solve simple separating (subtraction) problems in the classroom. Frequent usage will help them to understand the concept of and vocabulary used when solving separating stories.

Home Connection

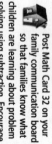

Post Math Card 32 on your family communication board so that families know what children are learning about problem solving using subtraction. Encourage families to work together with their child to solve similar basic problems at home, such as how many yogurts are on the shelf before and after somebody eats one.

MATH CONCEPT CARD
33
Problem Solving

How many apples are there in all?

LEARNING GOALS

Numbers
- uses concrete objects to represent sets

Problem Solving
- explores and solves simple problems

Math Vocabulary
equal
how many
in all
same number

Problem Solving

▶ Point to the baskets and ask: *How many baskets are there?* Count the four baskets with children.

▶ Point to a basket and ask: *How many apples are in each basket?* Count the two apples in each basket. Say: **There are two apples in each basket. The baskets have the same number. The numbers are equal.**

▶ *How many apples are there in all?* Count all eight of the apples by twos.

▶ Repeat, asking the question on the card. Call on individuals to point to the apples and baskets as other children count. Help children count to find out how many apples there are in all.

▶ Place the card in the Math Center. Children can use it to help explore similar problems.

Make It Easier Distribute two crayons to each of two children. Ask children to tell how many crayons they each have. Then ask them to count how many crayons they have in all. After children finish counting, count the crayons by twos to confirm their answer.

Make It Harder Challenge children to form several groups of two with objects such as bears or blocks. Have them count by twos to see how many they have in all.

Lesson Tips

- Use blocks or other manipulatives to show how four sets of two can be combined to form one set of eight. You can use baskets or other containers to recreate the problem and solution.
- Have children practice counting by twos during other classroom activities.
- Provide children with many opportunities to observe and solve simple problems in the classroom.

Home Connection

Post Math Card 33 on your family communication board so that families know what children are learning about problem solving. Encourage families to work together with their child to solve similar problems at home, such as counting pairs of sneakers or socks.

Problem Solving

How can you share these with a friend?

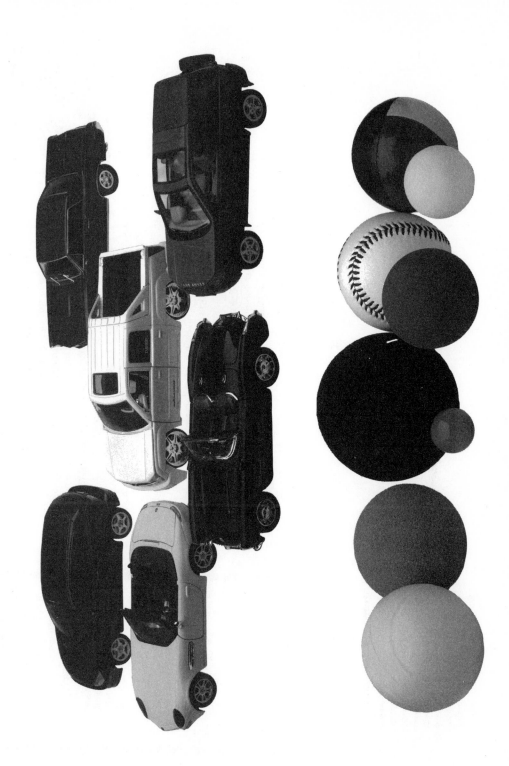

34

How can you share these with a friend?

LEARNING GOALS

Numbers
- uses concrete objects to compare sets

Problem Solving
- explores and solves simple problems

Math Vocabulary
equal
how many
in all
same number
share

Problem Solving

▸ Cover the balls in the picture. Point to the cars and ask: *How many cars are there in all?* Count the six cars with children.

▸ Say: **Let's pretend you want to share these cars with a friend. What can you do?** Elicit children's responses, and divide the cars as they suggest. Count the number in each group after each suggestion to check if each group has the *same number*. After children suggest making groups of three, say: **Now there are three cars in each group. The numbers are equal.**

▸ Ask the question on the card and then discuss how to share the balls with children.

▸ Place the card in the Math Center. Children can use it to help explore similar problems.

Make It Easier Give a pair of children four toy cars, four balls, or four blocks. Have them figure out how to share the toys so they each have the same or equal groups.

Make It Harder Gather a group of ten teddy bears or cubes. Challenge children to figure out how many groups of two they can make. Continue with other groups of cubes.

Lesson Tips

- Use sets of six toy cars and eight balls to demonstrate the problems. Have children divide the sets into two equal groups.

- Sketch the groups of cars and balls. Place different-colored tiles or counters on the subsets you want to form and count. This concrete visual will help children understand how to make groups of objects with the same number.

- Provide children with many opportunities to observe and solve simple problems in the classroom. Frequent usage will help them to understand the concepts and vocabulary of problem solving.

Home Connection

Post Math Card 34 on your family communication board so that families know what children are learning about problem solving. Encourage families to work together with their child to solve similar basic problems at home, such as how four family members can share eight biscuits.

Problem Solving